Fun Run
and other
o x y m o r o n s

F W

Praise for Joe Bennett

Fun Run and Other Oxymorons

Joe Bennett

Scribner

First Published in Great Britain by Scribner, 2000
An imprint of Simon & Schuster UK Ltd
A Viacom Company

All articles in this book have previously been published in New
Zealand in two books, *Just Walking the Dogs* and *Sleeping
Dogs and Other Lies*, both published by Hazard Press. The
articles which appeared in *Just Walking the Dogs* were
published between April 1997 and August 1998 in the
Christchurch *Press* or the Wellington *Evening Post* or the *New
Zealand Herald*. The author would particularly like to thank
Bruce Rennie of the *Press* for his encouragement and perception.

1 3 5 7 9 10 8 6 4 2

Simon & Schuster UK Ltd
Africa House
64–78 Kingsway
London WC2B 6AH

Simon & Schuster Australia
Sydney

A CIP Catalogue for this book is available from the British Library

ISBN 0-684-86136-4

Typeset in Sabon by SX Composing DTP, Rayleigh, Essex
Printed and bound in Finland by WSOY

Contents

Introduction

I have had it easy. I was born into the middle classes of southern England in April 1957. Precisely three months later, Harold Macmillan told my parents that they had never had it so good.

I have not fought. I have not suffered. Prosperity and peace deprived me of everything that gives a childhood zing. I was fed, loved and happy. I did not have to go to church or learn the piano. My father never lost his job, nor my mother her temper. I was only mildly molested by my cricket coach. I went to a good school, and a better university where I drank almost as much as was good for me.

Since then jobs have fallen into my lap. Lovers haven't, but when I stopped crying I found I didn't much mind. The jobs have been in various countries, but my address in all those countries has been Easy Street.

Since 1987 it has been Easy Street, New Zealand. I live here only because I haven't left here. It is in New Zealand that middle-age found me. It put a mortgage round my neck and dogs at my feet. Nothing is ever the place's fault, and the dogs delight me.

If anything holds these articles together it is that I like people but not in herds. I distrust all beliefs, most thought and anything ending in *ism*. Most opinion is emotion in fancy dress.

Language seduces me. I can sniff in the following pages the influence of numerous authors, most of whom hold strong opinions. When I read Evelyn Waugh I agree with him. But when I read Orwell or O'Rourke I agree with them too. It is not their opinions I believe; it is their style.

Most of these articles began as vague ideas or single sentences. As I wrote, the ideas changed. Sometimes the original sentence disappeared. What emerged often surprised me. If the words rang right or made me laugh I let them stay. As the little girl said, 'How do I know what I think till I see what I say?'

When I got stuck I took the dogs for a walk.

J.B., Lyttelton, New Zealand, August 1999

Tools for men

At this time of the year it is important to rake up leaves. If you leave them lying around, nature will rot them down into something useful. Since gardening is the art of messing nature around, that obviously will not do.

Today I saw a man attacking a pile of leaves with a thing that looked like an elephant's head with an engine. The engine roared, smoke billowed, and if he jammed the monstrous nozzle hard up against the leaves they rustled a bit. It was perhaps the most useless machine I have seen; and as soon as I saw it I wanted one.

In many ways it resembled a water-blaster. Any job a water-blaster does can be done in half the time with a scrubbing brush. But for a man a water-blaster beats a scrubbing brush every time because it's great for practical jokes and the opposite of a prostate problem.

Every tool, you see, has a job to do. That job is to confer status. Turn up at a working bee in a leather builder's apron with a battered twenty-four-ounce claw hammer dangling from the hip like a Colt 45 and people will see you as a man who knows. And as a man who knows you are entitled to spend the working bee drinking beer, giving advice, saying 'noggin' a lot and lending out your twenty-four-ounce claw hammer to stop it bruising your hip.

Jack-hammers, concrete mixers, road-drills – indeed all tools that require the use of ear-muffs – are desirable additions to the toolshed. Ear-muffs, of course, are not. Hearing is dispensable; status isn't.

Every man should also own a circular saw. It makes you screw your eyes up so you look like Clint Eastwood. Furthermore, no saw can match it when it comes to cutting through nails. There's something about the scream of metal on metal and the sheen of a well-halved nail that sings to a man's soul.

No man, however, buys a cordless rechargeable drill. He may be given such a drill for Christmas, but on Boxing Day he takes it to the builders' merchants as a down-payment on a real drill with double chuck, hammer action and a cable like a fat black snake. Such a drill has two handles so that it can and must be fired from the hip like an M-16.

Nevertheless, when handled properly almost any machine can become a good thing. For an example, as well-known man P.J. O'Rourke has observed, take the vacuum cleaner.

A man with a vacuum cleaner just has to discover exactly what the machine will suck up. Paper-clips rattle nicely up the pipe. Full ashtrays are fun. A merry gentleman of my acquaintance burned the guts out of three consecutive vacuum cleaners by cleaning out the grate with them. I admire that. He

4

convinced the manufacturers to replace the first one. The second two he claimed on insurance. I admire that even more.

All the same, when vacuuming, one should resist the goldfish bowl.

The most important man's machine is, of course, his car. Men need a Honda Civic; men want a Ferrari. A man's car has a short gearstick with a wooden knob, two seats, no boot and an acre of bonnet. The bonnet has the same psychological effect on men as the nozzle on the leaf-blower. On the distant tip of the bonnet is an upstanding bit of chrome in the shape of the maker's logo. This is circular so the driver can use it like a rifle-sight.

Beyond even the car is the nuclear ICBM. These have sadly gone out of fashion except in manly India, but ordinary missiles will do, too. Exocets, Sidewinders, Silkworms, Scuds – they're serious men's machines. They shift leaves.

The soul of the city

As the sage once said, 'The soul of any city is its park'. That sage knew his onions.

There's a drunk. At six o'clock on a Saturday morning in winter he shambles out of one of those exquisite concrete bunkers that dot North Hagley Park and heads for somewhere else. Through the darkness he bears an indescribable bundle and he grunts as he goes.

At the same frozen hour a tribe of scrawnies leap from their Merivale beds of Danish wooden slats. They pull on cutaway shorts and training shoes with a swoosh on the side and more technology in the sole than a Ford Cortina. Across Carlton Mill Road they bounce and into the frozen park. The drunk grunts.

An eerie half-light begins to wake the ducks. Round and round the park the scrawnies run, their scything legs like those anatomical skinless maps in podiatrists' surgeries. On their faces the mask of grim endeavour. The drunk does not acknowledge them. They do not acknowledge the drunk.

The sun peeps. It drives away the serious scrawnies, sends them bounding back to muesli and that green milk that has had the milk taken out. Their place on the running tracks is taken by the gaspies.

The gaspies are mostly male and mostly on doctor's orders. They do not like to run. Their shorts are sad things, the remnants of beach fashions from the seventies or from rugby when you could kick for touch from outside the twenty-five. The gaspies' only pleasure in running is stopping. They have little pumpkin bellies. Sometimes dogs accompany them. The dogs lean on trees smoking while their owners catch them up. As the gaspies pass each other, they smile the sort of smile that torture victims favour.

The sun is warming to its task. Enter the large women. The large women come in pairs. They wear weatherproof make-up and costly tracksuits. As they walk, they swing their arms as if trying to clear jungle. They also talk. And they have dogs which trot daintily but don't swing their arms. The large women exude happiness, but in due course, as the sun thaws the turf, the large women give way to the tiny sporties.

The tiny sporties wear rugby jerseys which they will grow into within a couple of decades. From a distance the tiny sporties look like little tents with feet. They don't play rugby; they play swarming. Somewhere in the swarm there may or may not be a ball. Every so often a rogue tiny sporty will break away from the swarm and score a try. It is the second half, so the tiny scores at the wrong end. There are tears. Mothers whose tracksuits testify to the elasticity of nylon envelope their offspring.

As the sun climbs the sky, the tiny sporties become medium-sized sporties with haircuts that look like accidents. The medium-sizers don't play swarming; they play swearing. But having sworn they too move on, taking their hair and vocabulary to McDonald's. They are replaced by the big and the serious, the ones who have at last grown into their rugby jerseys.

For eighty minutes of winter afternoon the park shudders and thunders. Then a whistle, cheers, and bedraggled dirty men head for an evening of beer and lies, leaving only a litter of insulation tape to clog the council mowers on the Monday morning.

The winter sun lowers. The air chills. Mothers with pushchairs flee the stretching shadows. A few scrawnies nip out for a last burst of scrawny relish. Night seeps into the spaces. The ducks swivel their heads into the world's least comfortable sleeping position. Knots of party-goers straggle through the park, pushing, laughing, loud in the great black silence.

Night has settled. The sexually dubious melt among the trees. Vandals push over the rugby posts. The Securicor car cruises with its floodlight, illuminating trees with criminal tendencies. Then in its unforgiving beam it snares a stooped and shambling figure coming from somewhere else. The figure grunts and bears his bundle towards a concrete bunker.

The soul of the city sleeps.

The bathroom floor

You may not have heard about it, but twenty years ago today I was thrown out of a squalid little flat in Spain for refusing to wash the bathroom floor. My argument, which I thought, and still think, a strong one, was that it would only get dirty again.

Since then I have learned that, for a man, keeping the bathroom clean is easy. You pay someone else to do it. If you can't afford that, you get married. It amounts, in the end, to much the same thing.

Keeping the body clean is less easy. I suppose you could pay someone else to do it, but if you pause to imagine only a cloth between the cleaning lady and your coccyx, you head for the shower alone.

The first law of the shower states that no two shower controls in the universe are the same. The second states that the temperature markings on shower controls bear no relation to the temperature of the water. The third states that, however much a shower control may rotate, the degree of rotation required to change from ice-cold to scalding is never more than one millimetre.

Years of research and millions of dollars have gone into perfecting a plastic that grips nicely when dry but is slippery when wet. It is used to make shower tubs. It kills people. They slip, they shatter a hip and pain immobilizes them. In falling, however, they have jolted the shower control just over a millimetre.

What they needed, of course, was a rubber bath-mat with vaguely obscene little suckers underneath, like the tips of those arrows that boys lick and then fire at windows and girls. Such arrows never stick but they are a satisfying means of distributing saliva.

Rubber bathmats, on the other hand, do stick to shower tubs. But peel one off – and what a deeply sexy noise that makes – and look underneath. What you're looking at is the birthplace of the Ebola virus. Penicillin doesn't come into it. This stuff's black. With feelers.

With showers so perilous, ordinary baths remain understandably popular. In the nineteenth century when people were smaller, baths were bigger. Now we're bigger, they're smaller. It's called progress. Submerge the shoulders in a modern bath and your knees rise like twin Krakatoas.

The first rule of the bath is that it is impossible to position one's head satisfactorily at the tap end. Go to the other end, however, and there's the problem of how to get more hot water into the bath without sitting up. The sort of toes we need got left behind somewhere in the climb out of the primeval swamp.

Taps on the side of the bath are not the answer. Baths are supposed to induce relaxation. It's hard to relax when the hot tap is gaping so close to your crotch that there's only a washer between you and a skin-graft.

Baths, however, are splendid for some things. The first of these is smoking, because a bath is a ready-made and efficient ashtray. They're also good for reading in – but not library books. Rule two of the bath is that library books fall into it. Rule three is, all other books do, too.

The only other source of water in the bathroom is the hand-basin, easily identifiable by the stains beneath the taps and the build-up of crud in the soap-holder that doesn't hold on to the soap. Hand-basins have uses, especially when the toilet's occupied, but they are not places to wash. Washing oneself at a hand-basin is simply a means of transferring water from a bowl to the floor.

Which, if I had only realized it at the time, would have solved my little Spanish problem rather neatly.

Beds

The recipe for good sleep is a bed and a clear conscience. Either ingredient can be replaced by gin. Gin has always been gin, and a clean conscience is still available to anyone who doesn't sell real estate, but beds have changed.

I had thought that a bed was anything horizontal and softer than the ground, but I thought wrong. Beds have become a mirror of the times. Whoever coined the name 'Beds R Us' may not have been able to spell but he knew a thing or two.

The bed of the eighties was the waterbed. Waterbeds had something. That something was smut. Waterbeds were the great blowsy whores of the bedding world; men liked them more than women did because they imagined romping in them. The makers of waterbeds knew that. They decked the frames in brothel velvet, and they padded and buttoned the headboards. In effect waterbeds were built of flesh; taut, tumescent and tactile.

When first I got the chance to sleep on a waterbed I was drunk. I found that whenever I moved, little ripples radiated outwards through the mattress. Then the little ripples radiated back. On the way they met more little ripples heading outwards. My head bobbed like a dinghy. Nausea rose. Suddenly I had no choice; I had to sit upright.

The scientific name for this sensation, incidentally, is 'the whirling pits', and at university I learned the cure: keep one foot on the floor. If you're drunk enough to get the whirling pits then you're drunk enough to sleep with one foot on the floor. In my day you got a real education at university.

But the waterbed was not just smut and ripples. It was also a womb. It cradled the sleeper like amniotic fluid.

In the frozen winter of 1991 I slept for three months in a waterbed beside tall windows overlooking Hagley Park. It was, I suppose, a womb with a view. Every morning I looked out from the warm embrace of water at the white expanse of park; every morning I had to wrench myself from under the covers and into the cruel air. I understood why babies wail when they are born.

Six years ago you could buy a sexy three-ton womb in every street in town. Waterbed City competed with Waterbed World competed with Wet Dreams Inc. Then suddenly the voluptuous eighties gave way to the Kate Moss nineties, and the womb-boom burst.

There is, they say, no accounting for taste, but clearly a herd-instinct lingers in the human mind. The typically melodious German word for it is zeitgeist, but I wonder if there is perhaps some term in physics to describe the sudden switch of polarity

13

that took us in no time from the self-indulgence of the water bed to the flimsiness of the futon.

The Japanese have always been minimalists. They cook fish minimally and grown minimal bonsai trees. They make wonderful minimal soups garnished with a single sliver of mushroom. They have, I am told, railway hotels that resemble mortuary filing cabinets. You rent a minimal drawer for the night and there you sleep on a futon, for the futon is minimalist bedding.

It is the bedmaker's dream and the sleeper's nightmare. It is the mattress you have when you're not having a mattress, and yet when the futon was chic the makers could charge what they wished. It was an expensive way of sleeping on the floor. Like nouvelle cuisine the futon is a con, and like nouvelle cuisine it has died. From its ashes has risen the Scandinavian slat-bed.

In unappealing Castle Lindo in Leicestershire I saw a bed that Elizabeth I is supposed to have slept in. It appeared to have slats across its base, but I realize now that it could not have done, because the slat-bed is as modern as dehumidifiers.

My neighbour has a Scandinavian slat-bed. She told me what a wonder it is. 'But,' she added, 'you have to have a really good mattress.' I asked why. She looked at me as if I were dandruff. 'So you can't feel the slats,' she said.

Slats will fall, of course, and something will rise in their stead. We, the buyers of beds, have three options: we can mock fashion, follow it or lead it. I have decided to lead it.

14

I am about to patent a sort of net slung between poles. I shall call it '*le hammock*'. It's cheap to make and seriously uncomfortable. It should go down a treat in the nicer suburbs.

Be the boss

Don't give in to technology. Stand up to it and beat it. Never forget that it is the slave and you are the master.

My bedroom light fizzled then died. I padded to the cupboard to fetch a replacement bulb.

One week and three trips to the supermarket later, I remembered to buy one. The dead bulb had held sixty watts, so I bought one containing a hundred. It should last almost twice as long.

I stood on the bed. Mine is a dead bed. It has sagged into the shape of a rowing boat. I straddled it, balancing on its gunwales with the ease of a trawlerman in a gale. I reached up for the light-bulb.

Raising both hands above one's head does little for the balance. It is why trawlers don't have electric lights. Nevertheless I removed the light-bulb. I did this by not letting go of it as I fell. The glass came away nicely in lots of little pieces. Some of them even had blood on them, making a decorative effect on my snowy bachelor bed linen.

Close technical inspection revealed that I had indeed removed the bulb. What I hadn't removed is what home handymen call the metal thing that fits into the thing. I headed for the toolbox for pliers.

One week and three trips to the supermarket later, I remembered to buy a pair of pliers. They were made in Taiwan with green plastic handles and they cost agreeably little. They were of a variety called 'Heavy Duty'.

I played trawlerman again. The thing that was stuck in the thing came out with a sharp crack. A chunk of the thing it was stuck into broke off. The pliers broke too. Undaunted I inserted the new bulb. It lit up.

A handful of working electricity unnerves me. I leapt down into the rowing boat, deftly catching the bulb as it fell. I turned the light switch to off, climbed back up on deck, slid the bulb in again and twisted it into place. It fell out. Peering into the thing I saw that the bit of the thing I had broken off was the bit of the thing that held the thing on the light-bulb in place. It wasn't just a light-bulb I needed. I needed an entire new thing.

One week and three trips to the supermarket later, I remembered to find out that the super-market doesn't sell things. I needed to go to a specialist thingmongers. I thought of getting a man in, but pride said no. The wallet agreed.

The man in the electrical bits shop smiled when I explained in technical terms exactly what I was looking for. It was the smile of one expert to another, a sort of electrical freemasonry. In no time at all he unearthed exactly the right thing. 'That's exactly the right thing,' I said. He smiled again and

17

both the other assistants smiled too. I liked the electrical bits shop.

Electrical repairs require one big decision. If you don't turn off the mains you risk death by electrocution. If you do turn off the mains you have to reset the clock on the microwave. And on the video, and on the oven and on the bedside table. I always choose death by electrocution. Apparently it's swift and you get to look like Rod Stewart.

Pausing only to write my will, I fetched a screwdriver from the toolbox.

One week, three trips to the supermarket and one to Placemakers later, I had acquired a gift-pack of fifteen screwdrivers with blue plastic handles. They were made in Taiwan. I was ready.

Our physics teacher was called Glegg. Glegg was strange. He told us that electricity consisted of a chap called Mr Volt standing in a box. Mr Volt spent his life pushing barrels out of the box and round a circuit. The barrels were called amps. I bore this in mind as I applied my screwdriver to the things that attached the wires to the thing. In the style of all good electricians I screwed up my eyes and stopped breathing.

Glegg also taught us that there were three wires. One was the live wire, one was the earth wire and the other wire was another wire. They came in different colours. I couldn't remember the colours.

It didn't matter. There were only two wires attached to the thing. Both were black. Electricity has obviously changed.

When I detached the broken thing the light shade

fell off with it. I put it aside and attached the new thing to the wire. It was easy. I inserted the light-bulb. It stayed inserted. Dismounting the trawler deck I started breathing again and turned the switch. The light went on. I tried not to smile. I failed badly. I wished I had Glegg's phone number. I went to put the light shade back. I found that to put the light shade back I needed to detach the new thing. I put the light shade on the floor and went to bed. Masterfully.

The birds and the bees

How lovely to see sex education back in the forum of public debate. I can think of no other topic that offers more scope for sounding off to absolutely no effect.

Sex and education came from different planets. Sex attracts children; education repels them. Bringing the two together is like mating a panther with a wart-hog.

Nevertheless, some people make a career out of telling children about sex. Such people come in two species. Those of the first species have severe mouths, spectacles and haircuts. They wield words like 'morality' which children find deeply moving. Those of the second species wield guitars. They smile a lot, congratulate themselves on their frankness, and sing songs with titles like 'I'm a Merry Condom'.

Both groups have a profound effect on adults; they induce horror and nausea, respectively. Neither has the least effect on children.

My sexual education counsellor was Dave Parmenter. Dave had Prince Charles ears, oddly shaped knees, and a knowledge of matters sexual that few eight-year-olds could rival.

Dave's sex lecture was thrilling and anatomically bang-on. He didn't say much about alternative lifestyle choices but he drew superb diagrams in the mud with a stick. I listened rapt and believed none of it. It was all too bizarre to be possible, so I sought out that wellspring of wisdom, Miss Truman, a turkey-throated 630-year-old spinster who taught us English and singing. When she sang her throat wobbled.

When I told Miss Truman what Dave Parmenter had told me, I don't think she believed it either. Briefly, and uniquely, I saw her throat tighten. It was only a glimpse, however. Once I had spat the soap out of my mouth Miss Truman told me to watch the birds and the bees.

So I did. I watched thousands of meaningful inter-avian encounters without learning much. The male leaps on the female amid a flurry of feathers, pecks her on the neck a couple of times and then flies back to the pub. If the earth moves, it does so with haste. Obviously thousands of men have taken the bird-lesson to heart.

The trouble with the birds, however, is that it's not all clear what's going on where it matters. One can understand why bird-watching becomes a life-long hobby and needs a zoom lens.

As educators, bees were even worse. I followed bees around for weeks without ever seeing any of them engage in meaningful inter-apian rumpy-pumpy. I have since been told that they sport in the privacy of the hive and the business involves

21

hundreds of males crawling over one fat female. Did Miss Truman know that?

There is nothing new under the sun. The same debate as is raging now was raging thirty years ago. As John Mortimer observed at the time, the young had suddenly discovered in the swinging 1960s that it was possible and fun to go to bed together. But, he added, they made the same discovery in the swinging 1410s.

Bomb the bastard

Bomb the bastard. Don't hesitate, devastate. Blast him, shoot him, crucify and nuke him, for I need entertaining.

Call off that Madeleine Albright. When you're talking war you don't send in your granny with the soft fat arms. Besides, there's never any point in bandying words with a bloke with a moustache who wears battle-dress in bed. Dust off Stormin' Norman and let's get cracking.

It's been seven long years with nothing decent on telly. I need a war. Remember those smart bombs that could turn left at traffic lights? Only problem in the last show was it was all in black and white, but they've had plenty of time to fix that. They've got a bomb now that's so smart you can show it a photograph of the target and it'll go find it. They should show it a mug-shot of the chief nutter himself and then let it loose to sniff round the presidential palace, trying the doorhandles, checking the cupboards, till it runs the dingbat to earth in one of his presidential lavatories and has him cowering up against his gold-plated Jacuzzi showing his teeth and promising to shave his moustache and marry a Jew, all relayed on prime-time through NoseCam to a global audience of civilized television-owning democrats which means us and we're all on our feet screaming 'GET THE MADMAN' and 'GIVE HIM ONE FOR ME' and then Whammo! it's time to crack open the bubbly. Beats *The Darling Buds of May*, though that Zeta something or other, she's a belter.

Great place to have a war. Miles away from any-one who matters. To be sure, the old fruitcake has got eight presidential palaces with more spare bed-rooms that you can shake a stick at and every one of them crammed to the ceiling with fifty-seven varieties of biological nasty while his harem has to make do with the servants' quarters, but if you think about it the whole place is surrounded by billions of miles of sand, so give it the Cruise missile treatment, I say. The stuff will all soak away in a year or two, and if a few camels come down with a dose of anthrax, well, frankly, who gives a monkey's? I've never seen the point of camels myself. Sandra went on one of those coach tours of the pyramids and she reckoned there was this one camel would bite you soon as look at you. It had yellow eyes, Sandra said. It used to spit as well. Yellow spit.

That nerve-gas stuff, too, if you think about it, it's all in our favour. One whiff of Sarin and you go all liquid inside and swell up to twice your normal size, and if you fall over you can't get up. So when Uncle Sam dumps the Semtex this stuff gets sprayed all over Baghdad and then when the Marines move in they find the elite Iraqi fighting force rolling

24

around in the dunes like so many Mr Blobbies. Apparently you can finish them off by just popping them with a pin. Great television. I think I'll get Sky; CNN's unbeatable on that sort of stuff.

So what's holding us back? Why aren't the boys out there in the Persian Gulf right this minute chalking skull-and-crossbones on the bomb-bays of the B52s? Scuds? Don't make me laugh. You don't make a serious missile and call it 'Scud'. Sounds like something left in the bath. Remember when the balloon went up last time all we ever saw of the Scuds was file footage of the things being carted around the desert on trucks and having nets thrown over them. They didn't even point up at the sky. And anyway, even if one of them did freakishly get off the ground and start homing in on Tel Aviv, the Yanks would have the whole place surrounded with those brilliant Patriot things that stand bolt upright like proper missiles and cost about three zillion bucks each. One hint of a Scud on the radar and every Patriot in the Middle East would spring to attention and blast the thing out of the sky before you could say 'Star-Spangled Banner'.

Sure, a few civilians are going to cop it but, as my old gran used to say, you can't make an omelette without a casualty or two. And to be honest, it might knock a bit of sense into the rest of them. I feel sorry for them in a way, those Iraqis, I do really. I mean they don't know any better, do they? They've just been fed a whole lot of lies from start to finish, all that business about the will of Allah, and American imperialist dogs, and of course you can't get Sky in Iraq, oh nosirree, every foreign TV signal is intercepted and scrambled at the border so all they get is *Your 101 Best Fig Recipes* and the local six o'clock news written by Saddam's rent boy.

I reckon that if you gave them half an hour of Judy Bailey and a couple of All Black Tests live they'd soon storm the presidential palaces themselves and have the divine leader dangling by his testicles from the nearest mosque. That would be okay, I suppose, as long as CNN got there in time.

Animal porn

Like you, whenever I hear the word 'pornography' I immediately think of Africa. And in particular I think of well-I-never, such-wonderful-photography-don't-you-think, and did-you-see-that-one-about-rhinos. Sunday evening nature programmes like *Our World*. They're filth.

David Attenborough's up to his nineteenth-century-explorer shorts in guano in the depths of a forest in Borneo or some other equally unspeakable part of Africa and he's smiling because he and his trusty eighteen-man camera crew, chef, twenty-six-wheeled air-conditioned bus, personal trainer and shorts designer have finally tracked down the almost-extinct Bornean giant leech. The said leech is at present battling the threat of extinction by sucking as much blood as it can out of David Attenborough's scrawny thigh in the time needed to get a few close-ups of its hideous proboscis, after which the personal trainer hauls the leech off with a sort of schlurpy noise and then stamps on it. If he's got any sense, that is.

But he hasn't got any sense, none of them have, otherwise they'd be sitting at home drinking beer and watching the telly and working for the Inland Revenue rather than hotfooting it after leeches.

But what really gets me about nature porn is the way they make animals out to be nice. Animals aren't nice. They're animals.

Somewhere on the plains of the Mekong Delta – don't expect me to be precise; Africa's all one to me – there's a woman in sweaty safari gear and no make-up whispering reverentially into a camera about a pack of cheetahs which she's been following around for three years now, and which treat her as one of the family – the odd one with no visible fur who always sits on top of an armour-plated Land Rover with a camera – and to which she has given names. There's Long Paws (after the play by Harold Pinter – literary in-joke. Ignore it) and Squat Face and poor little limping Diddums, and the big worry is whether Diddums the infant cheetah is going to be able to murder enough zebra to get him through the next rainy season. We all hold our breath throughout the rainy season which happily coincides with the ad-break.

But all that's actually needed to get weak little Diddums through the rainy season is for the grinning Yes-Massa driver to ram the Land-Rover into first and power away towards the fleshpots of Nbongo with enough force to dislodge nine stone of Little Miss Safari Suit from the roof and leave her squealing and alone under a vast and remorseless African sky to discover how Diddums actually feels about their really rather special relationship. What she will swiftly discover is that Diddums has got the emotional complexity of a kitchen appliance and great big teeth.

That, however, is the stuff of fantasy. Instead we get those magnificently phoney sequences with a snapshot of Diddums looking up and pricking his ears accompanied by a voice-over saying 'But suddenly Diddums catches sight of a movement in the undergrowth' at which point we cut to ancient file footage of a wildebeest. Meanwhile Yes-Massa has been despatched with a shotgun and returns with a sack of wounded wildebeest, which are then let loose at intervals until Diddums finally manages to nail one.

Which of course is why most people watch. They like the killing. The producers are perfectly well aware of this so they do all the slaughter in slo-mo. And it's always the good-guy animals that get to tear hunks out of the still-twitching bellies of the animals that don't look anything like the family pet and which are anyway so stupid and numerous that it doesn't matter if they die.

If you get sucked in by the inch-thick emotional loading of these 'programmes' try giving the wildebeest names. It all seems a bit different when the cheetah is burying its teeth into an oesophagus that belongs to Emma. Better still, call them all brutes and change channels.

Ah yes, but it's educational. Well, that's what they all say, in particular those bulky men in shiny tuxedos who stand outside places in Manchester Street smoking. 'Come on in, son,' they say, 'it's educational.' (Such men have a point of course.

Take the invitation and dance up those dimly lit red-carpeted stairs and you can learn a lot of good stuff.)

But you won't learn any good stuff from *Our World* even though it's fronted by the profoundly educational Richard Long. The reason you won't learn any good stuff is that it's all lies.

If you want to learn good stuff about, say, scorpions, get stung by one. That's exactly fifty per cent of everything you need to know about scorpions. The other fifty per cent is the best way of killing them.

It's napalm.

The essence of Sunday

When I was young museums were like Sundays
– oppressive, depressing and adult. Historically
museums have served several purposes within our
cultural framework. The first of these has been to
provide somewhere for tourists to go when it is
raining.

Obviously, however, museums have always served
one main purpose and for the well-being of our
society they must continue to do so. They hold
our yesterdays for the sake of our tomorrows.
Traditionally museums have been places to which
adults have brought their children in order to teach
them their cultural identity by boring them to a
coma.

The first essential of boring a child is silence.
Churches invented the idea. Libraries took it up.
Museums perfected it.

Silence delights middle-class, middle-aged adults.
It is the distilled essence of Sunday afternoon.
Nothing more thrills the adult soul than to stand in
raincoat, sensible shoes and silence before a well-
organized display of bird-skeletons.

In a traditional museum one is expected to walk

31

slowly, gawp and say 'Shhhh'. Adults like doing these things.

Museums further gratify adults by being educational. Educational in this sense doesn't mean that you learn stuff. It means that you can convince yourself that you are learning stuff. A typical educational activity in this sense of the word is thumbing through *National Geographic* for pictures of naked African women.

The sad truth is that for all their good intentions traditional museums are overwhelming. One marvels at this exhibit or that but learns little. There is simply so much to see, so much to read. Nine visitors out of ten emerge from a museum wondering quite what they went in for. The tenth is found at closing time snoring amid dinosaurs.

Children, of course, don't like to walk, gawp or be silent. They like to run, scream and break things. But because museums are meant to teach, and teaching is something we inflict on children, today's curator seeks to lure the child. His bait is the interactive exhibit.

In the local museum there is a wall of buttons with photographs of birds beside them. Press one of those buttons and reasonably soon you will hear the call of the bird in the photograph. It is a highly educational display. Only today, indeed, I saw a child with hair like a porcupine learn that if you press all the buttons at once you can make a lot of adults scowl at you as you run away.

There is also an artificial cave. Children crawl in one end and emerge from the other end. From this they learn that if you crawl in one end of a cave you will emerge from the other end.

I do not know what lurks inside this cave. I am an adult and so I don't do interactive stuff. I am afraid of looking foolish.

For this reason it was with nervous tread that I visited the Museum of New Zealand, the notorious Te Papa, for Te Papa is the home of interactivity. And how the children flock to it. Indeed one's first thought as one passes through the vast portals of Te Papa is what a lot of flocking children.

Te Papa has banished the oppressive silence of the traditional museum. When not making noise, the children are queueing to get into the seriously interactive things. It's remarkably similar to a cinema complex. They seem to like it.

For the adult the change from a traditional museum is equally startling since Te Papa denies any gulf between high and low culture. Working on the notion that everything is culture they have placed a 1960s fridge alongside a 1960s painting by Colin McCahon. I rather liked the fridge.

Te Papa has the world's greatest collection of escalators and lifts. As a learned art critic friend observed, one immediately gets that department store feeling; and with a skill one can only admire, the good folk of Te Papa have recreated exactly that talent of department store escalators and lifts for carrying you past somewhere you wanted to go to somewhere you didn't want to go and can't quite find your way out of.

Te Papa is the Museum of New Zealand. They

have sought to capture the essence of the nation, to hold up a mirror for us to see ourselves. In a curious sort of way they have succeeded.

Gone is that austere oppressive reverence that one associates with colonial New Zealand, traditional museums and churches. What has replaced it is the spirit of that modern place of worship, the shopping mall. Like a shopping mall it is full of kids and lights and a few things you like and lots of things you can't see the point of. Te Papa has a sense of energetic chaos.

It is glitzy, eclectic and unrefined. I don't think any more learning goes on there than in traditional museums and, though its intentions no doubt are scholarly, its mood is popular.

What Te Papa has done is to shift the idea of a museum in this country from age to youth, from seriousness to levity and, most importantly, from Sunday to Saturday. I rather like it.

The tongue-thing

So, the lassie has a thing through her tongue. It is a silver thing, a sort of dwarf weightlifter's dumb-bell, and she has developed the charming knack of making one end of it protrude between her lips and then wiggling it from side to side. Thus she has added her bit to the popular art of body-piercing, an art much practised among primitive peoples. Indeed the number of holes in this girl's flesh and the tonnage of silver bangles dangling from them may well denote high rank, but today I am concerned only with the dumb-bell through the tongue.

And I am not alone in being concerned with the dumb-belled tongue. The nasty principal of this girl's high school is also concerned with it, so very concerned that he has told her to remove it. She refused. He suspended her from school.

Enter the lassie's father, frothing with indignation as protective fathers of vulnerable children understandably tend to do. And, of course, he sat her down, told her in forthright terms to remove the dumb-bell, apologized to the principal and sent the lassie to bed without any supper.

Or so we would have supposed. But we would have supposed wrong. Instead, dear papa gave her a pat on the back and a tube of Brasso for the dumb-bell and then informed the fascist principal that his daughter would remove the dumb-bell only over dad's dead body, and while he was still breathing she would continue to attend school.

The nub of dad's argument was that the school had contravened an inalienable human right, the right of freedom of expression. His daughter wanted to wear the tongue-thing; the tongue-thing was, indeed, a profound expression of who she was, and the bossy little schoolmaster had no right to crush her individuality.

Well, now, it has been a hot summer. Let us suppose the daughter had chosen to attend school naked (except of course for the tongue-thing, which I would imagine is pleasantly cool in the mouth when the wind is from the nor-west). Would dear papa have let her? Would he have crushed her free spirit?

Or were she to decide to go to live with baboons in whatever ghastly country baboons live in, or to become pregnant, or to insist on eating only cat-biscuits, would papa nod his head, smile, pat her on the back and say 'That's my girl'? He would? Then he is nuts.

No doubt dad would argue that his daughter is doing nobody any harm by piercing and embellishing her tongue. Ignoring the possibility that she may not be doing her tongue a fat lot of good, on the face of things he would seem to be right.

But how faces lie. Let us consider the tongue-thing from the point of view of the school's principal. If he allows the father's argument and admits the right to the tongue-thing he will be in no position to reprimand any child who breaks any convention. Freedom of self-expression will be the catch-cry, and soon the principal will find himself in charge of a school where anything goes. Or rather he won't be in charge of it at all.

The result of that is easy to imagine. Parents will remove their children. The school will shrink and then sink and leave not a wrack behind.

We hear an awful lot about rights. Father insists on his daughter's right to express herself. At the same time he implicitly assumes her right to an education. Both rights are indeed enshrined in law in New Zealand. Neither is a natural right. Both are artificially created by an artificially organized society. They are not so much rights as privileges.

If dad is unconvinced by this distinction I invite him to send his daughter to North Korea, having first taught her a few choice phrases of self-expression about the president of that country. The authorities would certainly remove his daughter's tongue-thing. Whether they would bother to extract it from her tongue first is less certain.

Or let him send her to Eritrea to insist on her inalienable right to eleven years of education at the state's expense. They love a good laugh in Eritrea.

The rights that this gentleman is insisting on are rare in this world. Most people do not have either of them. They are to be cherished, and should not be invoked for the sake of an infantile whim. *De minimis non curat lex*, which translates loosely as 'Stop whining about tongue-pieces, darling, and thank your lucky stars you live in a wealthy democracy'.

And then finally there is the question of age. Father insists that his daughter knows best. At what age did she start knowing best? At fifteen, or ten, or five? Or was she pretty clued-up in the womb? And if she knows best, if she is capable of making adult decisions for herself, then what need has she for school? School is a place of training. His daughter does not apparently need any form of training. Whatever she does is right.

I have just discovered that one may not become president of the United States until one is thirty-five years old. The hoary old birds who knocked up the Constitution clearly thought that if you have lived that long you have enough experience to talk sense. How wrong they were. Witness several presidents and one New Zealand father.

House hunting

I am seeking a new house. All I have found so far is a new language. I have learned that sad little houses respond to TLC. I was glad to learn that you could make a house happy by hugging it. I had thought houses to be like lovers: hugs are all well and good but in the end they require a lot of money.

I have also learned about society. My mother sheltered me from riff-raff so I have never knowingly met an executive, but from the real estate columns I have discovered that executives don't live in houses. They live in residences. Residences cost several zeros more than houses, but they do have indoor/outdoor living. This is much better than having a garden.

Almost every building for sale that is not a residence is a wee gem. Villas ooze character, space and grace. Summerhill stone is definitely not a drive-by. Wherever I choose to inspect, viewing will impress.

Last weekend an ad for a cottage leapt from the page. I swatted it down and read it. The cottage nestled, apparently, in a secluded easy-care section. I saw hollyhocks and rambling roses, a woman in tweeds with a trug, quaint little dormer windows and, lying on the sun-drenched veranda, a fat tortoiseshell cat for the dogs to dismember. My cottage. I decided to view and be impressed.

As the dogs drove I lounged in the back seat of the turbo mega-butch, permanent four-wheel-drive, I'm-a-real-tough-cookie, all-terrain recreational vehicle, the sort of vehicle that growing numbers of all-terrain recreational women drive to the shopping mall. The treble overhead cam purred overhead like a tortoiseshell cat. With the dogs singing merry motoring songs I dreamed of my cottage life to come.

I had expected to be able to see my cottage from the road, but I hadn't expected to smell it.

Shielding my eyes from the real estate agent's grin, I emerged from the car. The real estate agent pumped my hand, stroked the dogs, introduced himself as Something Hook-Norton and handed me his card. I found I had erred. This was no real estate agent. This was a real estate consultant. I would have told him how honoured I felt had I been able to take the handkerchief from my nose.

The easy-care section was indeed easy-care. Ten square yards of concrete give little trouble. Fool that I am I had thought that cottages were built of weatherboard or gingerbread. This one was built of fibro-board and flimsy flat stuff. These are permanent materials. The windows were not dormer; they were broken. The exterior was painted a cheerful excrement brown.

The interior, however, was not so attractive. It

40

was built for dwarves with no sense of smell. There clearly had been a tortoiseshell cat, but someone else's dogs had got to it months ago and stashed the remains beneath the floorboards. Shortly afterwards its owner had joined it.

'What a wee gem,' said Consultant Hook-Norton. 'A bit of TLC and she'll be good as.'

Therapy

Therapy is in. Therapy is good. The Yanks got it first, but when the Yanks start scratching we all end up with psoriasis.

Just like you I want to go to a trim, mature, sympathetic woman in sharply cut clothes and just a hint of a middle-European accent, and I want to lie down on her couch and I want to burst into tears. 'Help me,' I weep. 'I am small and feeble and middle-class and pink. Help me.'

She says nothing.

I let rip. All my heavy stressed back-of-the-skull weight, I let it explode in her consulting rooms; I burst like a zit. Self-pity drips on to her neutral pastel carpet. The yellowness of my spine irradiates her neutral pastel walls.

She says nothing.

'For God's sake,' I scream, 'can't you see, it's all gone wrong. Therapist, mother, therapist-mother, mend my aching head, my fear, my crippled feelings, my dishonesty. Shake from me this dread. Let me step forth into tomorrow, bold and resolute and honest. Let me tell the man at the top that he should not be at the top. Let me tell the beautiful that they are beautiful. Let me hug children and laugh and sing at outdoor tables in the shade where the food is long and good and Mediterranean and fresh and where we sleep in the afternoon and wake easy. Teach me to live, earth-mother, let me be.'

Half an hour of this blubber and I feel just dandy. I bounce from the couch. I seize her cool hand. Then on impulse I hug her, feeling the little nobbles of her spine and the flattening of her breasts. I slightly dislodge her spectacles. She gives me a warm understanding smile. But she says nothing.

At a desk outside sits a young woman with a stopwatch and a calculator and a box of tissues. She presses the stopwatch. 'Thirty-three minutes today, Mr Bennett, at $7.50 is . . . let's call it $250.'

'Let's call it $300,' I sing, handing her crispies from the cashflow machine and snatching a tissue to give me sustenance for the windy street beyond. We part in smiles, she with the dollars and I with a pump in the heart and a mind as easy as thistledown.

It's called therapy. Anyone can do it. I've got a business plan. I'm going to start a therapy chain.

First I'm going to a party. I shall seek out the sad, the ones clutching a drink in both hands and taking an interest in the bookshelves. I sidle over, my sympathetic look worn like a badge, my eyebrows lowered at the sides and raised in the middle. Like a mournful, wondering labrador.

'Have we met?' asks the sad one, suddenly nervous.

I maintain my silence, my enquiring, sympathetic mournfulness.

'It's just . . .' the sad one begins, 'it's just I don't know anyone here, you see, and I don't seem to be very good at mixing, you know. It's always been like that. My mother used to say . . .' and they're away. I stand, I lean, I listen. I nod and I cluck and I listen.

When the tears start I press my business card into the damp hand, pat the wrist in reassurance and say, 'Just give my secretary a ring.'

From there it snowballs. The sad men and the sad women come and talk to me and feel better and pay me and tell their friends. And I never say a word.

Then I branch out. I make lifesize replica balloon 'me's and I plant them beside couches in offices in Los Angeles and Sydney. Balloon 'me's in Ulan Bator and Tashkent. I charge by the minute: $7.50 a minute to strip the emotional clothes in front of a balloon with labrador eyebrows. The McDonald's of therapy. We'll all be happier.

I'll be so rich I'll need therapy. I'll go to myself.

How to be famous

Andy Warhol painted soup cans. This made him famous. But Mr Warhol was of a generous disposition. He reckoned that in the future everyone would be famous for fifteen minutes.

Fame is seductive stuff, and though the paths of glory lead but to the grave, many of us still yearn for a posse of paparazzi, even if it is for just a quarter of an hour.

A glance at God's filofax might reveal, however, that you're booked in for your quarter of an hour at 4 a.m. on a Sunday, in which case you must take fate into your own hands.

The first step to fame is to get on to television news. An increasingly popular way of doing so is to acquire an Uzi and do target practice in public and on it. It doesn't matter where in the world you do this; the cameras will come to you. So, unfortunately, will the law.

A safer route to stardom is to arrange for a member of your family to die in spectacular fashion. The cameras will sniff you out as a grief-stricken relative, at which point you must be ready. You need a photograph album, the pages of which you must turn mournfully. Sobbing's a bonus, and so is a floral sofa, but never forget that in television terms grief means a photo album.

A slower but less drastic method of hitting the six o'clock screen is to dress up as a scientist. Television news works on the theory that no one can understand a technical item without pictures of a scientist doing something with test-tubes. What you do with the test-tubes is immaterial; it just has to look sciency. The investment – a white coat, inch-thick glasses, two dozen test-tubes, false beard (optional, but worth the effort, especially for women) and an Einstein wig – is nugatory. If you strike it lucky you could become file footage.

There's also a niche for those with theatrical gifts. Dress as a pantomime cow and slither around on wet concrete. If you manage a truly spongiform performance you might replace the clip of the stumbling heifer that accompanies any reference to mad cow disease.

At greater cost but with absolute certainty of televisual success, go to Bangladesh and wait for a disaster. You won't have to wait long. Within days a flood, typhoon or train-crash will wipe out a sizeable tonnage of local citizens. Hasten to the scene and just wait to be discovered. If you want top billing, smear yourself with blood from the carnage and put your arm in a sling. Working on the formula that one lightly bruised Kiwi has the news value of 4,000 dead Bangladeshis, you'll be a star. But do warn your relatives. The cameras back home will find them. They must have photo albums handy.

For the less adventurous the easiest way to the screen is through an animal. Take one dog and train it to befriend a pig, or else get your vet to make it cross-eyed – a simple and relatively inexpensive procedure, and he might throw in lop-sided ears for the same price. If you can then teach the mutt to howl in time to the Bee Gees, so much the better. The slot you're aiming for is the 'Ooh-aaah' bit after the weather, so cuteness is essential, sentiment everything. If your dog ain't cute, kill it. There's plenty more at the pound.

Your last resort is the weather itself. Don't imagine you have to know anything about anti-cyclones, depressions and isobars. The weather report is mainly devoted to telling us what weather we have just had. You will have to learn, however, to pronounce the names of towns in a way that none of the locals do, and you will need a wardrobeful of wacky ties and a fund of folksy humour.

If all this fails and you still want fame, try painting groceries.

Cars and frying pans

Cars are like frying pans. The key to both is to do nothing to them.

All food can and should be fried. The best frying pans are those big black French jobs that strain your wrists. In the hands of a trained chef they can kill burglars.

If you let such a pan mature, and in particular if you let a decent depth of fat develop in it, it will fry anything. If after several months the fat becomes so deep that you lose sausages in it, then the solution is to eat takeaways for a couple of days while the fat solidifies. It can then be turned out on to a plate and cut into squares. Crunchy Cholesterol Slice is its proper title, and it is best buttered.

The fatal error with frying pans is to wash them. Water affects their chemical composition, making the potassium ions covalent. This means that, after washing, the surface of the pan has thousands of microscopic hands reaching up like those waving sea anemones on coral reefs which are common on television but rare in Lyttelton Harbour.

Crack an egg into a washed pan and all the little hands will clutch on to the electrons in the egg-white. The egg will stick to the pan like superglue, the only difference being that the bond between the egg and the pan will be strong.

It's much the same with cars. I know quite a lot about cars. I know that red cars go faster than other cars and that men don't drive automatics. I know that driving fast is safer than driving slowly because an accident is a random happening in a random place and so the less time one spends in any random place the less chance one has of meeting the accident lurking there. I also know how to put petrol in, although not how to stop it regurgitating over my shoes, and I know that cars, like frying pans, work better if left alone.

But the society of meddlers has other ideas. Because my big red car is a few years old, the powers of this land, advised no doubt by the brown-suited troglodytes at Occupational Safety and Health, have decreed that every six months when the monster is purring with efficiency it has to be taken to a garage to be mended. This happened to me only two weeks ago. As usual they gave my car a WoF. As usual I gave them just under $1500.

When I got the car back it was immediately evident that they had done an awful lot of work on it. The driver's seat had been adjusted, no doubt to render the mechanic's weekend joyride more comfortable. The mirror had been adjusted too, presumably by the feet of the mechanic's girlfriend.

Further evidence that they had worked long and hard, so to speak, on my car was the fact that it wasn't going as well as when I took it in.

A glance at the docket explained a lot. For a start it explained why mechanics are all young. Having worked for ten years at that hourly rate they retire.

The rest of the docket had all the lucidity of the instruction manual to a Korean VCR. There were words like 'grommet'.

Anyway, true to the frying pan theory, a few days after the car had been fixed, little red warning lamps appeared on the dashboard. I found them quite decorative and ignored them. If you pander to a car's whims it will soon have you opening the bonnet every five minutes.

The car stopped. I turned the key. The engine made the noise of a man flicking through a telephone directory. Then it fell silent.

Now there are two types of car owners. The first type is those who left school early. Such people crawl under stopped cars, adjust the grommets, strip down the carburettor manifold, suck petrol through the sump gasket, spit it out manfully and make the car go.

The other type is the educated few. We are strong on the ontological insecurity of nineteenth-century novelists. When our cars stop we ring the AA as soon as we have finished crying.

My AA man was a charming chap called Chris. He opened the bonnet as if it was the easiest thing in the world, fiddled a bit, then did exactly what I would have done: he fetched a hammer.

At this point I offered to help. After all it was my car and if anyone was going to swing a few blows into the bodywork I had first claim. To my surprise, however, Chris tapped gently at a complicated bit of the engine. To my even greater surprise he didn't make the car start. I think Chris may have stayed on too long at school.

The trouble was the alternator. Obviously. Chris summoned an alternator man who soon told me all I wanted to know about the alternators fitted to Subaru Omegas, which was that they cost $150.

It was dark. I offered to hold a torch for the alternator man. He told me not to bother; he could change an alternator in the dark. And he did.

When I got home I fried some eggs, bread and peas and sat down with a nineteenth-century novel for a good long think.

Stealing the dead

That celebrated thief, an unidentified caucasian male, has strolled into the Auckland Art Gallery, brandished his equally celebrated weapon, a sawn-off shotgun (who does the sawing and why?), torn a painting from the wall, hacked it from its frame, run away and raised all sorts of questions about what is known as the art market.

The painting was by the unfortunately named Tissot, of whom none but the cognoscenti have heard. Tissot's greatest talent, which he shares with all our most valuable artists, is that he is dead. There's nothing like death to boost an artist's reputation. As Van Gogh discovered, self-mutilation is just not enough. You have to go the whole hog and keel over. Half a hog isn't much use, and a mere ear gets you nowhere.

The importance of death in art has been underrated, but the reasons for it are clear enough. It's all to do with economics. Dead painters stop painting. Thus the art market, that bustling throng of bored billionaires, knows for certain how many canvases the corpse has done and can be sure of the value of their investments. They know that if they invest in the dead they will not be faced with the sort of crisis that developed in the phone-card investment industry when a flood of new cards swamped the scene and so sadly turned money to mush.

A further advantage of dead artists is that they can be judged through the spectacles of history. Let us take Monsieur Tissot. Though born in France he inexplicably forsook the huge advantages this gave him with women and moved to England, where he changed his name from the romantic Jacques-Joseph to the rather less romantic James. In England he made a lot of money painting fashionable social occasions. Since then art critics have had a century or so to pin him down, and they have more or less agreed that he lies somewhere in the line of descent from Frith the realist to Whistler the a-bit-less-realist. In short, Tissot's been sussed.

Living artists are harder to suss. Living artists have the vexing habits of changing styles, producing too much and going out of fashion. Not many people understand modern paintings and fewer still like them. Even if they do, they depend on the critics to tell them which ones to like. To buy a modern painting is to gamble. The bored billionaires do not like to gamble. They like to win.

It seems to be agreed by the people who know – though how they know I don't know, and I do sometimes wonder whether they do know or whether they just like to be seen to appear to know on the principle that in the art world the appearance of knowing is more likely than not to be taken for actually knowing because everyone is desperate to know something for sure in this most subjective of subjects – that the unidentified caucasian male stole the Tissot (bless you) to order. The inevitable question is who issued the order.

Are we to believe that somewhere in the States or Switzerland or Saturn there lives a man – it has to be a man, doesn't it? – who is so rich, so lonely and so sad that he yearns to own a painting which he cannot display? Are we to believe that the passion for possession has so filled his soul that he will stoop to this? The answer would appear to be yes.

Is it for the beauty of the thing that the sad one has had it stolen? I somehow doubt it. Is it for its historical significance? I doubt that too. I suspect that, though he may not recognize this truth himself – for how could he live with himself if he did? – he wants to own it because it has an assured financial value and because if he owns it no one else can.

It is a further neat irony that by having it stolen, I guarantee our sad friend has increased its value. It is today a far more celebrated painting than it was last week.

I also bet that the Auckland Art Gallery has had many more visitors through its turnstiles since the theft than it did before. Art with sensation beats art for art's sake.

The urge to make art is fundamental to the human spirit. It is in many ways what makes us human. But there is nothing pure in human affairs. As this ridiculous episode confirms, vanity, greed, pretension and sheer sweet silliness flourish even in the world of art.

In his biography of Dante Gabriel Rossetti, the pre-Raphaelite painter, Evelyn Waugh, the greatest of twentieth-century writers (yes, he's dead), had this to say about some European travels of Rossetti and his pal Holman Hunt:

'They discerned "sweetness" in Fra Angelico, "coarseness" in Rubens, "power" in Leonardo da Vinci and "sympathy for sublime sentiment" in Titian – but no doubt they had a good time.'

I doubt if the same could be said of our sad billionaire.

How you can be as rich as Bill Gates

Bill Gates is nine times as rich as the government of New Zealand. Bill Gates is so rich that he gets to talk to President Clinton. Nevertheless there are advantages to his wealth. For example Bill Gates never wears a tie. Appearing before Clinton less than fully clothed has its dangers, but Gates didn't get where he is today by ducking danger.

The good news, however, is that where Bill Gates has trodden you can tread too. Stick with me and I'll show you how.

But first, let us consider what it means to be that rich. When Bill Gates gets money from the cashflow machine he doesn't check his balance first. Nor, when the cashflow machine is pausing, does he hold his breath. At the Lucky Seven lottery outlet he buys a whole roll of those scratch-and-win tickets and then pays the girl behind the counter to scratch them for him with that dinky little clover-leaf on a chain. Paradise.

In the restaurant Bill Gates has a starter and a main. If he feels like it he has that crayfish dinner for two without worrying if anyone else wants it. He doesn't bring a carrier bag full of warm white wine to a BYO restaurant, and when the bill comes he doesn't get out his calculator and check the menu to find the price of Sharon's crème de cacao which came with a little umbrella but, Sharon said, tasted of petrol. And when he's halfway down the second bottle and just beginning to feel the wind in his conversational sails whereupon the goody-two-shoes waitress minces over and hisses that there's been a complaint from table four and would he mind turning it down a bit, he buys the restaurant and sacks her. Think of being Bill Gates.

On aeroplanes he travels first class which means enough legroom for a dropsical millipede, seats that go horizontal, no queues for the toilets, prettier stewardesses who do up his safety belt, an overhead locker to himself, *Titanic* rather than *Home Alone 9*, screw-top bottles of French wine, thicker sick-bags and getting off first.

And think of Bill Gates's house. He's got an *en suite* bathroom and a walk-in wardrobe and a dehumidifier in every room. All his kitchen appliances are by SMEG because of the evocative name and the sexy European styling, and the dishwasher is the same colour as the cupboards so he can pretend he hasn't got one. On the deck there are hundreds of genuine Italian terracotta pots and a barbecue with one of those hood things over it and racks and a rotisserie so that he can cook whole fish perfectly every time as well as the sausages. And when he holds a barbecue he can absolutely fill his garden with those flare things on poles. Heaven.

Bill Gates's car says DOHC on the side and no one dares pronounce it 'dork'. He locks it with one of those beeping remote things which he can programme to play 'Baa Baa Black Sheep'. There's a dodecahedronic stereo with a 350 CD selector in the boot, and it's got 350 CDs in it, and he can open his garage door from anywhere in a twenty-mile radius with a device which turns on the light in the garage at the same time and kills burglars.

And think of being Bill at the supermarket. He just waltzes past the specials and buys huge bleeding hunks of fillet instead of that quick-fry string-vest stuff. And Bill simply heaps his trolley with the very best freeze-dried instant coffee in those fancy jars instead of that powdered own-brand muck which tastes like vacuum-cleaner bags and comes in plastic packets that split when you open them, and even if they do split on him he doesn't have to try and sweep the stuff off the kitchen bench and back into the packet, he just buys a new house and starts filling it with de-humidifiers.

When Bill gets the *Innovations* catalogue in his morning paper he doesn't have to read it. He orders one of everything. Three days later a parcel arrives with electronic golf-ball washers, an entire home gym and a solar-powered thing for storing shoes. Think of the fun.

Salivating? Want to know how he did it? I'll tell you.

Bill Gates thought positive. He made damned sure at the outset his Attitude was Pointed in the Right Direction. He knew that if he believed it he could do it. He organized himself a Dynamic Thought Pattern and he chose to be the Managing Director of his Own Life. He knew there was no such thing as a dumb idea. He began each day with a Motivational Monologue, did a Supermemory course during his lunch-hours and never went to bed without reciting his Success Inventory. Bill Gates set goals.

He got it all from a little book. It is called *Your Route to Wealth, Health and SMEG*, and is available from all good self-improvement bookshops. Even if it doesn't work for you, think of the purchase as your good deed for the day. Its author is starving.

Biplane or piggybank

Baby animals play games. Baby snakes play sweet little crushing-each-other-to-death games and baby lions play let's-rip-throats. The games teach the youngsters to be as vicious as their parents.

Young human beings do the same. The game they play is called Monopoly.

Now I gather that the makers of Monopoly wish to add a new playing-piece to the board. They have offered three prototypes – a biplane, a piggybank and a moneybag. They will choose, I guarantee it, the biplane. That way they will be able to continue to pretend that the most popular board game in the world for the last fifty years is just a harmless bit of fun.

To succeed in Monopoly you need greed, malice and luck. The money starts to trickle in. You corner a market. The trickle swells to a stream. Wealth breeds wealth. The stream becomes a Niagara. Once you've got the lolly, you are king and nothing holds any fears, not even jail. You just buy your way out. It's called capitalism. It's also called fascism. In the Soviet Union it was called communism. Perhaps we should just call it people.

Few joys compare with watching the dice carry a friend to your square which seethes with hotels. Friend has to mortgage his property portfolio and give you the cash. You grin. He's crippled. He ekes his life out for a few more throws and then you kill him. It's a laugh a minute.

The game inevitably ends with two tycoons lumbering round the board like dinosaurs, fixing each other with a flat dead eye. For them the world has shrunk to a board awash with property. It's Kerry Packer and Rupert Murdoch, each with enough dollar bills to light cigars for the rest of their lives.

But neither cares for money now, because they have seen through money. They know that money is just a token for something seated even deeper in the soul. That something is power. The dinosaurs circle, eyeing the jugular, probing for the chance to kill and so to reign alone, to become lords of all they survey: Mobutu, Marcos, Stalin, Ozymandias, master of the universe.

But the tycoons are blind. For when the death-blow comes and at last the victor stands alone he finds he stands atop a heap of rubble. The board has lost all meaning. Someone tips it over. The tokens of power jumble into nothingness. They are just plastic toys and bits of coloured paper. The master of the universe feels robbed. This is not what he wanted at all.

He stamps his feet. He wants another game. He rushes over to the window and shouts at the kids in the yard to come and play again. They are happy on their bicycles. They ignore him.

The bicycle game looks such fun. The master of the universe lusts to join it, but the others have glimpsed the malice in his soul. They will not let him play. He begs. He wheedles. He tries to bribe them. They laugh. The master of the universe bursts into tears.

Mum emerges to see what all the fuss is about. Mum is the Commerce Commission, the United Nations and God. She tells the children to be nice to each other. Sulkily they submit. For a while. Then someone suggests a game of Monopoly. Eyes light up.

Monopoly is us. That's why we like it. To put a piggybank or moneybag on the board would be to admit the true nature of the game. I bet you they choose the biplane.

The boys from Brazil

There's a town in Spain called San Sebastian where the Basque separatists used to murder a lot of policemen. It's a beautiful place built around a bay called La Concha. At low tide the sea empties from La Concha, and on Saturdays all the men and all the boys of San Sebastian stop murdering policemen and run out on to the beach to scratch lines in the sand, put up goals and play a soccer tournament. Teams win, teams lose, legs snap, nets bulge, players hug and players weep, and then the sea returns and the players pick up their goals and go home. The sea erases the lines and irons the sand and until next Saturday La Concha belongs to the fishes.

This weekly tournament at San Sebastian is exactly like the World Cup. It differs only in scale. Like the World Cup it seems to matter hugely at the time, but it proves ephemeral. When Brazil have won the World Cup and all the hugging and weeping have died away, the tide of oblivion will sweep back in, leaving only litter on the terraces and a few Englishmen too drunk to know it's over.

Soccer is the greatest of games because it is the simplest. It is the game one instinctively plays with toddlers on the living room carpet. Add an offside rule, a few billion spectators and an official snack bar and you've got the World Cup.

All you need to play soccer is a ball, and because the ball is round chance plays little part. What emerges is character. To play good soccer you need youth and skill. To play sublime soccer you need to be born within shooting range of the equator. Your skin must be the colour of milk chocolate or olives. You must also have only one name and it must end in 'o'. Ronaldo, for example.

Or Pelé.

In soccer it does not help to be white. I have just watched Holland play Brazil and none of the white Dutch players had names ending in 'o'. Their names all ended in 'donk' – apart, that is, from the chap whose entire name was Jonk. Jonk and the donks – now there's a name for a band – never had a hope. They played fine football but you could see that they were trying. What they sweated was sweat. What the Brazilians sweated was *eau de framboise au chocolat*.

The Dutch played as a team. They brought the ball upfield in beautiful neat triangles. They did what they'd been taught; but the Brazilians did what they felt. It was science against art, industry against genius, life insurance against love, beer against wine, Land-Rover against Maserati, Protestant against Catholic, northern cloud against southern sun. And the sun won.

Not that the Dutch didn't have their moment. Two minutes from time their svelte black centre-

64

forward, donkless of course, rose like a cobra and headed home as sumptuous a goal as you could wish to see. But only because the Brazilians let him. They were enjoying themselves. They wanted extra-time.

In the end, of course, it came down to penalties. I went to make coffee because penalties are taken by individuals. As individuals the Brazilians could not lose. I heard the cheers from the kitchen.

Brazil will win the final 2–0 but that doesn't matter. For the ninety minutes that the game lasts they will create an ephemeral beauty that will make the world gasp. After that someone will take the goalposts away and in will come the tide and the little pecking fishes.

Testosterone and tonic

Roll up, roll up. In the tent to your left, the bearded lady, to your right the rubber man, and dead ahead, sir, the fattest woman in the world. Roll up, roll up.

Those were the days. I would have rolled up to every freak show going. But nowadays the circus tents are empty. The freaks have stolen away to an even bigger circus. The freaks are playing sport.

I do not understand sumo wrestling, but I just love the wrestlers. From their dinky pony-tails to their dinky bare feet, they were made for staring at. I love those breasts like hammocks of squid, those barrel bellies, that shire-horse collar round the midriff with its worrying dangle of spikes, the audacity of those bared buttocks like the rinds of vast cheeses, those ridiculous legs, puckered monsters of cellulite atop ballet-dancer ankles.

Sumos live, I gather, on sumo battery farms tended by little monks who groom them and grease them and above all feed them. I love reading lists of what the sumos eat: six bushels of rice, a hundred eggs, a cow.

Of course, the most fertile sporting field for freaks is the USA. Not so long ago a gridiron team featured a character called The Fridge. He was considerably wider than he was tall and he ran like a garage. The Fridge was cool.

Basketball's good, too, except they're all so tall you forget how tall they are. If I was in charge of basketball I would make it a law that every team had to field one short chap to remind us how tall the tall chaps are. The best basketball team ever was the Chinese Olympic team of a few years ago. Four of their five players were minuscule, but somewhere in the forests of Szechuan the authorities had found a freak. He could barely run but he dwarfed buildings. So the tactics of this wonderful team were for one player to dribble the ball around in buzzy little circles while the rest of the squad helped the arthritic colossus up the court. Once they'd stationed him beside the basket, buzzy little dribbler lobbed the ball towards the ceiling. The vast one lazily plucked the ball from the air and dropped it through the hoop.

Now, it is obvious that so long as the rules of any sport favour freaks, then that sport will be beset by drugs because drugs can aid freakishness. It is equally obvious that the war against drugs cannot be won. The drug-makers are driven by wealth and glory. The poor old drug-detectors are driven only by a sense of fair play. Wealth and glory will win every time.

So why not let them win? Let them create the freakiest freaks you ever did see by shaking up every narcotic cocktail they wish. Steroid Stingers, Barbiturate Bombers, Testosterone and Tonic, let them go to it. Let the giant pharmaceuticals compete to sponsor the pharmaceutical giants.

The result will be a glorious parade of freaks for me to ogle at. It will be like the Olympics of the seventies when the East German chemists cleaned up every strength event going, apart from the women's shot-put. The latter was invariably won by the Russian chemists who had created two magnificently hairy sisters called Press. When the Presses won they wept. A thimbleful of their tears could defoliate a Siberian beech-forest.

We are constantly told that international sport these days is a global circus. Let it be a circus, then. And for those of us who do not want to pervert our bodies for a little ephemeral glory, we can continue to play beach-cricket badly for the fun of the children and not care who wins.

Moose-hunting by supermarket trolley

It's one of those Sundays. You know how it is. One of those Sundays when you can settle to nothing and the neighbours are playing the Bee Gees' *Greatest Hits* at full volume and the wasps of irritation in your skull say turn the telly on. So you do and there's a woman wearing a pair of athletic shorts that shouldn't be legal and she has come all the way from Latvia to New Zealand to throw the hammer. The hammer isn't a hammer, you understand, but more like one of those things used to fell mammoths from a safe distance, though it might as well be a hammer for all the good it does mankind, not that you particularly want to do mankind any good because mankind means huge women from Latvia, commentators who think hammer-throwing matters and people who like the Bee Gees.

So you zap the telly and pick up the paper only to discover that a supermarket chain has decided to make you pay a $2 bond on your trolley because they, poor dears, lose 200 trolleys a year and each one costs $350. At that price you immediately decide to become a trolley manufacturer and then equally immediately ditch the idea because it would lead to impossible conversations.

'Yes, that's right, yes trolleys, you know, for supermarkets . . . no, I don't expect you have . . . well, you sort of get some wire and sort of bend it . . . yes that's right, three good wheels and one spastic one . . . no, actually it isn't easy to make them stick together like that . . . ha ha, yes, mating, yes that's very funny . . . well, actually, about $350 each . . . well, it wouldn't be a very good second-hand car for $350, would it . . . yes, I know, well you can always take a basket.'

But what I really want to say is that the trolley bond will put paid to moose-hunting. Well, not exactly hunting, I suppose, more like moose-finding-by-chance. In Canada – Banff to be precise – on a skiing trip with Dave Collier way back in the days before mortgages and lady Latvians.

The *après-ski* at the Silver Dollar Bar and Grill has gone with a swing and about midnight we find a supermarket trolley in the street. Dave says get in, so I get in. Well, I've always been what mothers call broad in the beam, so there I am, wedged into the belly of this trolley with feet over the front and head up against the kiddy-seat and absolutely no chance of getting out without help and what with the ice on the street and Dave full of Labatt's it's a bit like the two-man bob and in ten seconds we're up to thirty miles an hour. Suddenly I see this neon motel sign with a sort of silhouette in front of it and it looks like the gigantic head of a . . . 'Stop!' I scream and

Dave digs the heels in and says, 'Why?'

'Look,' I say, 'Moose.' And he says, 'Where?' and I say, 'There,' and he says, 'That's not a moose,' and I say, 'It is so,' though I don't think it is any more.

So Dave biffs a snowball at it and it turns its antlered head, bellows a sort of uniquely moosey bellow and comes charging up the street towards us.

Friendship's a great thing. Dave and I grew up together. We were inseparable. One rapidly approaching suburban moose, however, and we have discovered the joys of separability which is fine for Dave who's off up the street like a man being chased by a moose but less fine for me who has a beam wedged inextricably in the belly of a supermarket trolley. Hooves are thundering my way and I'm trying to lever myself out and wondering whether Canadian supermarket trolleys are crash-tested against 2,000 lbs of moose flesh with horns and deciding they probably aren't and I'm wrestling and struggling and the trolley is rocking and then ever so slowly it just topples over on its side. But my beam is still wedged so I curl like a caged foetus and pray like billyo and good old god or rather God makes the moose thunder past and head on up the street after Dave.

'Get him!' I scream, and then, quickly, 'Sorry, didn't mean it,' because I don't want him or rather Him to change his mind and make the moose do a 180.

But now, I suppose, with $2 bonds on trolleys no one will leave them around any more, so yet another source of fun will dissolve in what is becoming a puritanical world, but at least moose will be able to browse in peace.

Meanwhile gangs of horror-children will hang around in supermarket car-parks with their skateboards and their hideous haircuts and when some poor pensioner wheels the groceries out to the Honda Civic: Whack! it'll be a skateboard on the bonce and a horizontal pensioner and the kids will be off with the trolley, and all for two lousy bucks.

So I suppose the supermarket will have to hire car-park guards, and what better than a vast lady Latvian with a penchant for hammer-throwing? The urchins will evaporate, and if some itinerant moose happens to wander into the car-park she could let rip with the hammer and a great Latvian grunt and take its legs out from under it.

Dave got away, by the way. He always did.

Erratum

Due to typesetting difficulties the word 'France' was repeatedly mis-spelt as 'Brazil' in the column on the World Cup. My apologies.

Fun and games

In the town where I was brought up all games took place at the recreation ground. Indeed it held something for almost everyone; the recreation ground was virtually a metaphor for life itself.

At one end stood the kiddies' playground, hilariously close to the main road, where junior citizens amused themselves by falling off the swings on to the concrete that the council had thoughtfully laid beneath. Next to the playground stood the War Memorial Gardens, to which the kiddies graduated when things began to happen to their bodies. Teenage couples would disappear into this dense and litter-strewn shrubbery for lengthy games of doctors and nurses. When they emerged they got married and joined the cricket club.

The cricket ground, of course, lay beside the War Memorial Gardens, and it was into those gardens that every local batsman strove to hit the ball. It was revenge for lost youth.

Into the rhododendrons went the ball and out came a yelp. Moments later there would scurry from the undergrowth a girl in a state of partial undress pursued by a boy in a state of complete frustration. On a fine day in high summer one could sometimes flush out as many as three couples with a single lofted on-drive. It was like dropping a ferret into a rabbit warren.

The target for batsmen at the other end was the bowling green. Land a cricket ball like a mortar in the middle of the bowls players and shortly afterwards you heard the ambulance. Clutching their tickers the ancient ones fell in concentric circles as if the ball was the epicentre of a nuclear blast.

The bowls players, however, never minded being used as targets since before their bodies betrayed them, they too had played cricket. They accepted the transition from hunter to hunted as part of the great scheme of things.

They knew, as well, that bowls wasn't a sport, but rather a pastime. It got them out and about and gave a little gentle exercise to withered limbs. Furthermore it staved off the day when they would toddle across the road from the recreation ground for the last time and pass through the grim portals of the Adastra Rest Home.

From there, it was just a short totter to the premises of Guttam, Washam & Plant.

Once upon a time, then, a thoughtful young man could stand with chin in hand beside the recreation ground and see his life mapped out for him from playground to graveyard. It was a strangely comforting vision, like the rhythm of the seasons. It sang of continuity.

But how all that has changed. The old certainties

have crumbled, and one of the first to go was the game of bowls. Despite being designed as the simplest and gentlest of games to allow for the frailties of age it has been hijacked.

These days the oldies can only stand aside and gawp as fit young things in tracksuits strut around the green and run after their bowls and squeal with excitement and care who wins. Such people are graverobbers. They will come to very sticky ends, of course, but that does little to console the elderly whose gentle recreation has been taken from them.

Of course, once bowls had become a professional sport, the dam of common sense had burst and the waters of absurdity flooded through the breach. These days it is possible to earn one's living from playing darts, or snooker, or water-skiing, or ten-pin bowling, or any one of a thousand brands of motor-racing, each as hideous and senseless as the other.

Who pays these people to play their games? I cannot tell you. Who watches them play? I cannot tell you. Where will it end? I cannot tell you that either. All I can tell you for sure is that with the bowlers of today and the fish-throwers of tomorrow walks the strange and spectral figure of the twenty-first century.

The anagrams of God

I, too, am a victim. The dog was asleep when my tennis ball stopped beside it. The dog woke to find me apparently making a grab for its testicles. It bit my wrist. I was seven years old, and so, as it happens, was the dog.

The dog's owners drove me to hospital in their admirable open-topped MG and bought me a Heart ice-cream which I'd never had before because they cost a shilling. I presume I had a tetanus jab but don't remember it. But I do remember spending the rest of my childhood rolling tennis balls hopefully towards sleeping dogs.

Last week a dog killed a man. The anti-dog lobby has gone rabid. With just the sort of cool, detached reasoning that did so much for Yugoslavia, they are slavering at the bar of public opinion and calling for fierce new laws to quell the canine menace.

In search of the true scale of the problem I studied a recent issue of the local newspaper. It contained thirty-seven accounts of human misery. These I divided into four sections: misery caused by people; misery caused by God; misery caused by dogs; and misery caused by goats. People beat God 34–2. The dogs failed to score. The goats notched a single spectacular goal.

My dog Jessie loves everyone. Jessie even loves golfers. In the urge to serve the merry golfers of Hagley Park, Jessie will leap into the rough to retrieve their muffed drives. The merry golfers roar like stags and wave their graphite shafts. And well they might, because the golfers of Hagley Park know that golf matters; some of them indeed have handicaps comfortably under thirty. Not for them the cheerful self-deprecating laugh. One of them once took to Jessie with a four-iron.

You see, the dog-haters and the Tiger Woodses of Hagley have something in common: they've got the world sussed. They know what's what. They are civilized and they have got it right. The rest of creation has got it wrong.

Dogs merely sleep and eat and love their owners. Dogs play games but they don't fill out their scorecards properly and they forget who won. They show enthusiasm and they shit without embarrassment. They own nothing and like sex and never hold grudges and love to serve and are grateful for all affection and don't judge. No wonder the four-irons scythe the air. No wonder people hate dogs.

The irrefutable statistical truth is that if something kills your child, that something will be a person or God. Not a dog. The one case brought against a dingo was thrown out of court.

Admittedly goats do get the odd child but not enough to be statistically significant.

Mankind invented virtue. We have built pulpits

from which to preach forgiveness, loyalty, honesty and love. Yet if we anatomize man our scalpel discovers vanity, acquisitiveness, deceit and golf.

I have not met a vain dog, nor an acquisitive one, nor yet a deceitful one, and only a few who play golf. Dogs forgive. They are loyal. They are honest. They love. And for the very few who are bad there are already perfectly adequate laws to control them.

I would point out to the dog-haters and the hackers of Hagley that there are five anagrams of God and surely it is no coincidence that one of them is ogd. There's also dgo, gdo and odg. I have never owned any of these.

But I have owned dogs. My dogs know nothing. Unlike me they don't imagine they know anything. My dogs are happier, better and wiser than I shall ever be.

Communing with shags

I've never had any time for the sceptics of this world who don't believe in telepathy. Life, you see, is contact with people, any sort of contact. 'Only connect,' said E.M. Forster. And if you think that's hooey, try playing the hermit for a fortnight and then get back to me. Or rather don't.

But if life is all about contact, what do you do when your telepathy is picking up only static, the e-mail has crashed, the letter-box is empty, everyone you ring is out or dead or both and there's a knock at the door from Sister Solitude and her pale and silent daughter Loneliness? I don't know about you, but I go and look at shags. There is solace in shags.

'Come on, dogs,' I say and we bound to the door, our tails walloping the crockery.

Round Lyttelton the shags roost in a couple of clifftop conifers, and very decorative they look, too, with their plump white breasts, one to a bird, and their necks like those bits of plumbing under the sink.

But it is not for their looks that I visit the shags, nor for the way they gurgle like outboard motors, nor indeed for the comfort of their brute insensibility. I go to laugh at them for being called shags.

They bring to mind a boy I went to school with called Tinker, which may not be the best of surnames, but there are worse, several of which end in 'bottom'. Tinker, however, was christened Simon. There are worse names than Simon too, but few worse than S. Tinker.

Then there was the little Egyptian boy whom I taught and who was called Fallik. He was only seven, the poor dear. And so very cheerful. It made one weep.

Anyway, off to the shags we go for a giggle, and it's a wild night. Clouds scud, trees thrash, and King Lear would have felt at home. The dogs disappear into the bush in yelping pursuit of imaginary prey, the night swallows them, and I am alone among the thrashing trees and the scudding clouds and the eerie dark.

I've always been a gutsy bloke, especially when alone in the bush on stormy nights, so even though I can hear the footsteps of an axe-murderer on the path behind me I just chuckle a nonchalant chuckle and carry on shagwards with my pulse comfortably under 200. And there I am, humming a catchy little Leonard Cohen number about suicide and the sea is crashing at the foot of the cliff and I'm thinking thoughts when *whoompha*, SOMETHING comes flying out of the darkness, headbutts my thigh and disappears over the cliff to certain death.

I react calmly. It is the work of only a few moments to locate my heart under a pittosporum, dust it off and slip it back in. Then I gather my wits. A couple of the more timid wits are gibbering behind boulders, but when all are safely gathered I set about seeking a rational explanation of the assault on my thigh, and of course there is a rational explanation; viz., I have just been attacked by an alien.

Well, good to have sorted that one out. The walk ends without further drama. Naturally, however, my mind chews over this encounter with a thigh-butting kamikaze Venusian.

And I recall a story I heard the other night from a learned gentleman in a hotel on the Lyttelton waterfront. It is a story of Russian science. (Be patient now; this will all come together.)

What the clever Russians did was to take half a dozen baby rabbits on a cruise to the bottom of the Baltic Sea in a submarine. Then they killed them.

Meanwhile, and here's the cunning part, up on dry land, other Russians sank electrodes into the mother rabbit's brain to measure the synaptic polarity of her ganglions. And sure enough, as each of her little brood was garrotted fifty fathoms below decks, there was a measurable discharge of protons. And if that doesn't prove the truth of telepathy and I don't know what else, but probably homeopathy, I'll eat a sceptic's hat.

Lyttelton is currently home to a sad gang of Russian sailors stranded here through no fault of their own. And I have no doubt that in their sadness they often take a stroll along the cliffs to cheer themselves up with a treeful of shags.

One thing I have noticed about Russians is that they look remarkably like human beings. So, from about 10 a.m. most days, do I. The point of all this is that down by the cliffs on a stormy night, what with the clouds scudding, trees thrashing, etc., it would be easy to mistake me for a Russian. And that, of course, is exactly what happened.

The thing that assaulted my thigh was no Venusian. It was a rabbit. A rabbit, furthermore, which was telepathically aware of the cruelties its fellow rabbits had suffered on the other side of the world and which was bent on revenge against the race that had done it to them.

Although the rabbit failed in its mission, and may well have perished, I think it all rather moving. Here was a rabbit that connected. Here was a rabbit that felt itself to be a part of the greater scheme of things. Here was a rabbit that laid down its life for its friends. Which of us can lay his hand on his heart and say he does not envy that rabbit its fate?

Life is contact.

P.C. Sturrock

On the morning when both my dogs were simultaneously, spectacularly and indeed voluminously
sick in the car, police buttocks shone from the front
page of my newspaper. And all this at a time when
the police were marching in search of a pay rise. It
would have been easy to conclude that the world
was coming to an end.

Now, there are several points that need to be
made here, but first, for reasons that should become
clear, I need to introduce you to a boy with whom
I went to school.

This boy had all the charm of dog-sick. He wore
shorts in the fifth form. Nobody else did. It was
agreed among the schoolboys of England that to
wear shorts beyond the age of twelve was a sign of
effeminacy, lunacy or both, which was exactly why
this boy did it. He longed for people to say, 'You
are wearing shorts, which means you are an
effeminate lunatic,' because then he could kill them.

He terrified me, and even now I hesitate to name
him. But perhaps at forty it is time for me to take
my spindly courage in both hands. His name (come
closer now; I am typing softly) was Sturrock.

Sturrock's greatest pleasure was Bawden. Bawden was a skinny child who never once called Sturrock an effeminate lunatic. Nevertheless, Sturrock regularly used to cram him into sports lockers the size of nesting boxes. On more creative days he would casually tie Bawden's limbs into a knot and place him on top of a cupboard like an ornament. When the ornament squealed Sturrock grinned.

At the end of the fifth form Sturrock decided there was little fun left in stirring the rubble of Bawden's psyche and he left school in search of fresh woods and pastures new. Driven no doubt by the wish to continue beating people up without being punished for it, Sturrock applied to join the police force.

Now, I do not know whether Sturrock became a copper, but for the sake of Great Britain I hope he didn't. Sturrock was not the sort of human being who took kindly to being asked the time.

Which brings us to the question of what sort of human beings police officers should be. The answer to that is extraordinary people. Armed only with the right to use the minimum force required to uphold the law, they are required to walk towards situations that instinct tells them to run away from.

They are required to accept insults but not bribes, to do as they are bid whether or not they agree with the instruction, to treat people whom they do not like in exactly the same way as they treat people whom they do like, and as a matter of routine to deal with the sordid and the sad, the brutal and the make our own fun, but more because it has something to do with the end of a year. Tonight at midnight the globe's odometer ticks over a notch and it matters.

Here in the port tonight those people who can wrench themselves away from *The Moira Anderson Hogmanay Special* will tour the pubs. There are several pubs here. In them will gather a cosmopolitan mix. There will be gold-toothed Russian trawlermen smelling of the fierce disinfectant used to kill cockroaches on board their awful ships. There will be Koreans and Vietnamese, wharfies and rugmakers, *émigré* artists and Arthur the beekeeper side by side in a seething mass.

A billion words will be shouted or slurred across the tables awash with slops. Few of the words will be heard but that doesn't matter. It's the doing of it that will count, the being there.

I am told that when women share a house, their biorhythms gradually merge until eventually they find they are all pedalling their menstrual cycles in time with each other. So it is with the revellers at New Year's Eve in the port. As the evening wears on, this ruck of humanity becomes like a school of fish. It develops an unconscious group will. Without anyone saying anything, all the revellers decide at more or less the same time to move to the next pub. One minute a bar will be bulging till its walls groan; the next it will be a wasteland of glasses, ashtrays and nobody. If you get out of phase with the mob you wonder if you've got the date wrong.

bloody. At rugby matches they must stand with their backs to the game.

In other words, they are required to behave unnaturally. They are paid to embody our better selves, to represent our civic conscience, the side of us that knows the way things ought to happen, to enforce the laws which we have elected people to parliament to make. Having a police force is like paying someone to make us keep our New Year resolutions. They are not paid much to do it. And it cannot be much fun.

And then, behold, on the front page of the paper, a photograph of policemen having a lot of fun. In order to raise funds for their Dragon Boat team they are stripping off mock uniforms to the delight of a sizeable crowd.

The obvious point is that the police officers concerned were off duty. At work a police officer is required to be as rational as Mr Spock. Off duty he is allowed to have red blood in his veins; he is allowed to love and to laugh and to drink and to be wrong. And if he wants to remove his clothes in a nightclub for a laugh, I am not at all surprised. It might help him tomorrow when he has to deal with someone who prefers removing the clothes from other people and then raping them.

Without the police the world would be an unfair place. If tonight the police all folded their tents and crept out of town, looting would begin within the hour, John Citizen would buy a gun tomorrow morning, the suburban vigilantes would be formed by afternoon tea and by lunchtime on Friday there would be anarchy. You and I, dear reader, could be dead.

In most countries of the world, the police are corrupt. Here, on the whole, they are not. No doubt the New Zealand police force contains the odd Sturrock but by and large the police act as they should; they guard the system by which we have chosen to govern ourselves.

In sum, then, the fuss over the strip show is wrong-headed and the fuss over pay is important. The police should be paid what they want and then some. The profession of policing should be so attractive that good and talented people queue to enter it.

Then when Sturrock emigrates to come looking for me and decides to do a little policing while he is here to keep his hand in, the recruiting officer can show him the door. With any luck Sturrock will kick it, whereupon he will be arrested.

Meanwhile, if you are seeking a Subaru Omega in good running order and fragrance is not a consideration, I might be able to help.

The ods roll over

As a child my main joy was watching the car odometer. Of course, in those innocent pre-metri days we called it the milometer; back then w barely knew what an od was. Nevertheless, what craved was that moment when the odomete numbers all rolled round together to produce a row of zeros.

Not daring to blink, I would follow the odometer's slow progress through the 990s. I would urge my father to drive faster, but he would decline on the grounds that top gear was for hooligans.

In the end, of course, it turned out like the weather forecast. Just as, however closely you listen to the weather forecast you always seem to miss the bit you want, so somehow I always seemed to miss the great odometer roll. One moment of distraction and 999.7 was suddenly 1000.1.

Immediately I would order my father to reverse. He would refuse, partly because he didn't believe in pandering to children, but mainly because he despised reverse. He called it the foreigners' gear.

Why do I mention all this? Partly to show modern youth that in my day we knew how to

As midnight looms a crowd gathers at the corner of Oxford and London Streets. There is a sense in the air of something important, something ritualistic and significant. A ship's siren blasts the night. A cheer erupts, and the people join hands to sing 'Auld Lang Syne' with such tunefulness that every dog in town joins in.

Then it's hugs. Some hug only their lovers; others, like random octopuses, hug anyone within range; while a few sly youths hug the girls they've spent the past year wanting to hug. And that is apt because New Year's Eve is a vent for feelings that spend the rest of the year deep in the burrows of reserve.

The mob drifts apart. Those who threw away their cigarettes at midnight nip back to the pub to replace them. Those who emerged from the rusting trawlers return to them singing. Those who came down from the hills stumble gently back up towards home. Halfway up the slope they may pause to catch breath, and perhaps, encouraged by the twinkle of the lights and the dark of the sea and the black presence of the hills, they will reflect on the passage of time, the year that has gone, the year that is to come.

For that, I think, is what this ritual of New Year's Eve is all about. It is a marker-post stuck down at random along the great amorphous road of time. It serves the same function as a birth or a marriage or a death. And like those occasions it arouses sentimentality.

For some that sentiment is the mawkishness of

televisual Hogmanay; for others it's the euphoria of the hug; for me I'm afraid it's a grim little poem.

> Life is mainly froth and bubble.
> Two things stand as stone:
> Kindness in another's trouble,
> Courage in one's own.

Every New Year's Eve this hideous doggerel rises unbidden to my mind. And every year, softened by beer, I resolve that henceforth I shall be kinder and more courageous. And having so resolved I meander the last few ods to home and grateful bed.

The resolution, of course, comes to nothing, but it's the thought that counts. Happy New Year.

Drinking rituals

Life is a sentence punctuated by rituals. The only thing the rituals have in common is drink.

The weddings start at somewhere around twenty and go on for about a decade. Of one's friends it tends to be the sexually avid who marry first. Two days after he left university, my mate Freddy, as groin-driven as any man you could hope, or possibly not hope, to meet, married a monoglot Pole. He didn't want conversation to interfere with the true purpose of marriage.

The wedding was a magnificent affair. Boat-loads of bulky Poles came over for the binge, bringing with them a serious devotion to having a good time and a solution to the language barrier. This solution came in several crates of clear bottles with handwritten labels. Over the course of a weekend so memorable that none of us can remember any of it, I learned more than enough Polish to get by in Poland. The Polish for vodka is '*vodka*'.

Joy was so utterly let off the leash at Freddy's wedding that it not only carved holes in the liver but also rather spoiled me for subsequent weddings.

Nevertheless it established a pattern that proved true of them all.

Every wedding bears an undertow of grief to which women are more sensitive than men, perhaps because they know more about affairs of the heart, or perhaps because they are more likely to be sober. It's something to do with the unmarried ones wanting to be married, and with the knowledge that the newly-made wife has got a lot of work in front of her taming the beast to whom she has now hitched her wagon.

Parents are always sad. If the tosh about not losing a daughter but gaining a son-in-law weren't tosh they wouldn't cry so much. Daughter is firmly lost and the son-in-law has the table manners of a skunk. Had daughter not developed an inexplicable and undissuadable crush on the thug they wouldn't have given him houseroom.

The critical moment at a wedding is the departure of bride and groom swamped with hugs, flowers and smut. Someone has tied cans to the car. Beer cans. Symbols of bachelorhood. As the car pulls off they rattle at the back of the groom's skull like the tug of the past, like the tinkle of the gaoler's key. Just round the corner the car stops and he leaps out to detach them, having first checked that there is no beer left in any of them. There isn't. Life has changed.

Meanwhile back at the ritual the women wave at the invisible car for about two hours and then turn to look at each other, a sisterhood of wonder. The men do the same, except the wave lasts two seconds and the look one. Then they sprint to the bar. Now's the time for some serious wedding.

As the years pass the invitations dwindle. The last pair of your acquaintances to marry are the bookish sort. She wears hairgrips, he a cardigan. It is a quiet affair. There is parsnip wine, but not enough to dull the pain.

After the weddings come the christenings. These are splendid bashes, which the children are mercifully still too blob-like to ruin. Women compare husbands and babies; husbands compare baldness. Hooch flows almost as strongly as the lies about the past.

The only downside to christenings is godfathership. God and fatherhood are among my weaker suits and yet several friends have asked me to do the job. I presume they imagined I would be good for presents. By now they know better.

As one descends into middle age the rituals drop off. For a while. But I got an invite this morning in a richly thick envelope. The card inside had a black deckle edging. I hope there will be drink.

Fine words, coffee and parsnips

Since Roman times they've been saying silly things about wine – *'in termino vanillae et tarmaci hintus'**, that sort of stuff – and no one has paid any attention. Wine has continued to do its principal job of making you say regrettable things at dinner parties. Now, however, and this is serious, the high priests of pretension have got their claws into coffee.

Coffee is a simple thing and good. Of a morning it prises apart the eyelids and unbends the fingers. At work it soothes the troubled breast. It makes the ideal accompaniment to fifteen cigarettes. It's bad for you. These are great virtues.

But now there is a bafflement abroad. I quote verbatim a conversation recently overheard:

Waitperson: 'Welcome, sir, to our unpretentious brasserie somewhere in the trendy bit of the city. My name is Gustave. I am your waitperson for today. You may admire my pony-tail. What can I do for you, sir?'

---

*'in the finish a hint of vanilla and asphalt'.

Jurassic Man: 'A cup of coffee.'

Waitperson (*barely suppressing a giggle*): 'I beg your pardon, sir.'

Jurassic Man: 'A cup of coffee.'

Waitperson (*patronisingly, for it has now dawned on him that he is dealing with Jurassic Man*): 'Do you perchance mean a Latte with an acute accent, sir? Or perhaps a Cappuccino with a random number of *p*'s and *c*'s and a sprinkle of cinnamon to disguise the flavour of coffee, which barely exists anyway because of the three inches of industrial froth. Or perhaps a Short Black is what you seek, sir, with or without racial jokes. Or maybe a Long Flat White, sir, a name we used to ascribe to a tall drunken friend at university. Or yet again you could be after one of those little French thimbles of Espresso Palate-stripper.'

At this point Jurassic Man realizes he has several options. Option one is to insist on just an ordinary cup of coffee, in which case he will receive the bitter dregs from a Cona machine last operated on Monday. Option two is to strike the waitperson. Option three is to stand on his dignity. Standing on the dignity is hard work when in need of a cup of coffee, but it does grant a good vantage point from which to strike the waitperson.

They've sunk their claws into food, too. Have you read the menu? There's poetry there. You used to get pork. Now it's *medallions* of pork. This translates as much less pork than you'd like. You are consoled, however, by the hint that the pig served valiantly in the war or won the pole-vault at school.

Further consolation comes from knowing that the dead pig is comfortable. No longer does it come with rice. It now nestles on a *bed* of the stuff, snoring gently no doubt and dreaming of storming machine-gun posts or soaring over the bar against a cloudless sky to the ecstatic grunts of a worldwide television audience of a billion sows.

To pamper it yet further while nestling on its *ris*, the pig has been drizzled with a warm *jus*. I like the sound of that. I'm going to hire someone to come to my bedroom nightly and drizzle me with warm *jus*. I shall charge people to watch. Perhaps the watchers might like to contribute by brushing me with a coriander and honey glaze. I shall reassure them that neither the glaze nor the drizzle of warm *jus* will affect my flavour in the least. Only my price.

Vegetables have gone, of course. The three veggies of yesteryear now arrive as *polenta*. That translates as a mess. Or a *roulade*, meaning a mess. Or a *terrine*. That means a mess. Or a *compote*. That means a compost. My primary school lunch-lady had mastered the *compote* in the early 1960s. She called it mashed swede. Dave Collier used to sneak it out of the dining hall in his pockets to throw at buses. A well-aimed handful could cover a whole windscreen.

As I say, wine's fine. They can say what they like about wine. But it seems that now, like the Anglican church, the pretentious are no longer content in their traditional temples. They are aiming for out-reach into the community. They are not welcome.

96

In the end, it all boils down to words. He was a wise and good man who said a long time ago that fine words butter no parsnips. He might have added that they make a lousy cup of coffee.

Nothing doing

At this time of the year letter-boxes and television screens are awash with advertisements for holidays. All of them are advertising the same destination, that eternally attractive location called Somewhere Else.

The attraction of Somewhere Else is that it isn't where you are. In Somewhere Else there is always heat, sand and a girl in a white bikini. Where you are there is cold, concrete and the extraordinary woman next door.

The girl in Somewhere Else spends most of her time swimming in limpid lagoons. She always does the breaststroke. Advertisers seem to like the way that makes her legs move. The woman next door has never been known to do the breaststroke. She does not look as if she would be very good at it.

The point about Somewhere Else is that when you are there you don't have to do anything. In Somewhere Else work is something that other people do. The idea of such indolence appeals to us.

Unfortunately, doing nothing is only interesting when there's something you should be doing. If I have an article to write or a pile of exercise books to mark there is nothing so delicious as slumping in the armchair with my feet on the windowsill and gawping out of the window. Clouds become fascinating. Once the words are written or the books marked, clouds are clouds.

In Somewhere Else your job is to lie on the beach, drink things with umbrellas in them and look for the girl in the white bikini. Ten minutes of this and you've found out that the things with umbrellas in cost a lot of money, your skin is reddening nicely, the sisters of the extraordinary woman next door have chosen the same place as you to go on holiday and are indeed proving that the family cannot do breaststroke, and the girl in the white bikini isn't there. Perhaps she has gone on holiday. In fact, she is probably looking for someone like you in the place you have just come from.

You turn over to cook the other side of your flesh. There's a faint tearing sound as your skin separates from the nylon lounger and you realize with stunning clarity that you're bored. There are ten days of holiday to go.

I met a mother of six the other day. She's one of those wonderwomen. While nursing a sick child under one arm and arbitrating a squabble between two others, she's cooking fishfingers for the horde and preparing chicken chasseur for an adult dinner party after the kids have gone to bed. In her spare moments she runs an employment agency.

On Mother's Day this year her family presented her with a week's holiday in Fiji. On her own. She burst into tears of gratitude, hugged each of them for five minutes and said she didn't want to go.

They wouldn't hear of it.

Before she went she crammed two weeks' work into one week to make sure everyone could survive her absence. When her family put her on to the plane she was exhausted. Nevertheless she spent the flight worrying. Somewhere over the Pacific she seriously considered going to the cockpit to tell the pilot to turn around. Taking a grip, she convinced herself that things would be better when she arrived.

On her first day she swam, played tennis, went pony-trekking and thoroughly cleaned her hotel room. On the second day she hung around the crèche until someone asked her if she would like to lend a hand. On the third day she came home.

The lure of holidays is the lure of fantasy. What spoils them is the one item of luggage that no one tells us to pack but which we carry with us everywhere we go.

The discontent of our winter

I'm a rudely healthy chap but once a winter I wake to a wet pillow. It happened last week.

During the night, fluids I couldn't name and didn't want to had seeped from my head. In addition, a tadpole had lodged in my throat, a tadpole that grew within hours into the mother of all frogs with a croak like a V8. By lunchtime the cold had blossomed into a phlegm-fest.

The cold may be common but it brings with it a vocabulary of rare beauty. Consider the congestion of catarrh. Or the music of mucus. Or the slither of sputum. And is there a more wondrously ono-matopoeic word in the language than phlegm? With its cluster of slimy consonants and its brilliant silent g, phlegm sings of ill-health.

At this point I would like to stress that neither I nor any member of my immediate family has ever expressed the opinion that Mucus, Sputum and Phlegm would be a good title for a firm of solicitors.

I live most of the year without sinuses. Then suddenly I have them to burn, and every one a phlegm-factory on overtime. The more I clear their product the more I encourage them to act as the source of the great grey-green greasy Limpopo River.

Nevertheless there are joys to having a cold. The first of these is that I cannot taste my own cooking. You can't imagine the relief. Furthermore a cold permits me to tell people I dislike to keep their distance.

On top of that I know I am losing weight. At peak production I must be evacuating half a pound of phlegm an hour. If I remember to take my handkerchief out of my pocket before I step on the scales I start thinking that two more weeks of ill-health and a really good toupé and it may not be too late for a career on the catwalk.

When a cold's at its height it takes about ten minutes to turn a freshly laundered handkerchief into an inexpressible horror. Screw it into a ball and throw it away. Well aimed it will take out a plump pigeon on the wing. Alternatively you can throw it at the wall. It will stick.

Best of all, a cold offers an excuse to visit the pharmacist, the health professional you see as rarely as possible because he failed to get into med school. Pharmacy shelves are crammed with essentials like apple and collagen skin revitalizer in tiny pots at hilarious prices. Perhaps to give the impression of clinical cleanliness, pharmacies are always overlit. They remind me of pathology labs on television detective series, in which laconic morticians chew meatpaste sandwiches while pointing out the angle at which the blunt instrument pierced the liver.

If science has not yet discovered the cure for the common cold, someone forgot to tell the pharmacist. He devotes a whole wall to cold cures. These come in two types: aspirins and fancy aspirins.

Aspirins are just aspirins. They are cheap and plentiful.

Fancy aspirins are just aspirins too. The difference is that fancy aspirins come in bubble packs so that you get bored trying to take an overdose.

Fancy aspirins are supposed to be easy to swallow. The price isn't. But as my grandmother always used to say, a drowning man will clutch at a bubble-pack.

Every packet of fancy aspirins has a pseudo-scientific name, a monstrous advertising budget and very few pills. You pluck one from the shelves which you think you may have seen on television. You associate it with a catchy little tune. The blurb promises it will soothe the throat, clear the nose, quell the fever, stop the shakes, find you a lover, pay off the mortgage and reconcile India with Pakistan.

It also promises not to make you drowsy. I don't know why. When suffering I would like to be drowsy. Ideally I would like to be comatose.

In the end you settle for the one that describes your symptoms best. On the pavement outside the shop you read the recommended dose and double it.

The irritating thing about medicines is you never know if they're working. For one thing you're not sure if you're feeling better because you can't remember how you were feeling before. And if you are feeling better you don't know if it's because of the medicine. I always feel the need for a spare body to act as a control.

Regardless of any medicine a cold is like a flood. For two days the torrent rages. Then there's a week of mopping up. It's one of the rites of winter. On balance I'm pleased to have suffered one. Like all illnesses it reminds me how lovely it is to be well.

Being a tooth

If Louis Armstrong were to breeze in here right now and sing 'What A Wonderful World' I would set the dogs on him. I've got toothache.

I normally cope well with pain. I can watch a batsman being hit square in the box and hardly even wince. But when, as now, it's 2 a.m. and my tooth has sent me to the all-night garage for Panadol and to the cupboard for Scotch and it's a hot night and moths are assaulting my face in their unnerving frantic fluttery way and the waves of pain in my tooth advance and recede like the sea, then I cut a less impressive figure.

There's nothing worse than toothache. Well, death is worse than toothache and so are most American situation comedies, but toothache can make a man desperate. It can also make a woman desperate. Dave Collier spent a year pursuing a woman called Delia. Delia was supposed to be of loose virtue but it always seemed to tighten up when Dave was around. Then, quite without warning, she leapt into his arms one evening and made smoochy noises. In the smug morning Dave asked her why the sudden change of heart. 'Toothache,' said Delia with memorable simplicity. 'I needed something to take my mind off it.'

Dave never found out if he had managed to take her mind off it because Delia ditched him that morning, but at least it proved, as Dave put it, that abscess makes the tart grow fonder.

W.H. Auden got it right about pain. When we're sick the world shrinks to the part of us that is sick. Nothing else is. Other people, as he puts it, 'are remote as plants', which is perhaps why hospital visiting is so difficult. The visitor and the patient inhabit different planets. The visitor comes from 'the common world of the uninjured' while the patient lives in the tiny world of his pain. The visitor cannot share this world, for 'who, when healthy, can become a foot?' Right now I am a tooth.

Dogs are far better at pain than we are. Injure a dog and it yelps once, then gets licking. Dog saliva seems to cure everything. It should be sold in pharmacies. I wonder if I can induce one of my dogs to lick my tooth. Perhaps I could smear the tooth with dog food.

Dogs, of course, have the advantage of being able to lick virtually every part of themselves. It's an enviable talent. Even if my saliva were as potent as theirs I wouldn't be able to cure anything except my forearms, my knees (just) and the edge of my armpits.

Toothache has one inevitable and terrible consequence. That consequence is dentistry. I am not what one would call a brave man but I have done some brave things: I have played rugby and twice I have almost made a tackle; at the agricultural show I stood quite close to a sheep for a photograph; once, near Paris, I defended a tent against a pig. When doing all these things I trembled and I sweated, but never has my back arched in terror as it does when my sweet, balding dentist reaches for the drill.

Instantly I look like the Sydney Harbour Bridge. The only parts of my body touching the chair are my heels and the back of my head. Then he switches the drill on.

Its whine is like that of the midnight mosquito which divebombs the ear. And with that whine comes the sort of smell that haunts war veterans. It is the smell of bone-smoke.

One of my former dentists used to hire a special nurse for my appointments. She was brawny. She had made money wrestling. Her job was to pin me down with a grip learned from SAS magazines while simultaneously swabbing my incandescent forehead and battling to keep the sucky thing in my mouth. On one occasion I bit her. She loved it.

But right now, the whisky has worked its whoozy wonder. The dentist can wait; sufficient unto the day is the evil thereof. I shall try to sleep.

Postscript

I love the dentist. He forsook golf to come in on a Sunday morning. Half an hour ago I left my pain and much of my wallet in his surgery and skipped down his stairs with a heart full of daffodils.

Right now the birds are shining, the sun is singing and I am sitting at a merry Cashel Street café, sucking the deep air of liberty, smiling at the painless world and supping at a cup of the frothiest coffee. The coffee dribbles instantly from the sagging side of my mouth to the trousers below. And I just don't care.

Pull up a chair, Satchmo, the dogs are friendly.

Just walking the dogs

Somewhere along the way I seem to have got the wrong idea about massage.

For me the word conjures up the image of an elderly businessman lying on a bench in a sauna while another man attacks his back in the manner of a chef chopping onions. Then the elderly one gets up and jumps into a cold pool. Shortly afterwards he is fished out, given CPR and sent back into the business community with a spring in his ventricles.

But I have just been told that this is not massage at all; what I have described is apparently a Turkish bath, thereby adding further mystique to a race whose most celebrated leader was called Kamel and who make a delight that doesn't.

My informant tells me that true massage is an altogether nicer thing. True massage apparently soothes the soul, untangles the tetraceps and induces a glow of well-being – like a sort of hands-on gin.

All of which is well and good, but in these rancid times one has to pity the true masseur. Fired with a need to knead he works his way through massage school – turn hard left between acupuncture and aromatherapy – buys a shop, a couch and a flagon of oil, erects a neon MASSAGE sign and sits with hands atwitch to wait for the knotted world to knock on his door.

And knock it does. Knock. A man enters. Knock; another man. Knock, knock, knock; man, man, man. And all too soon our rubber and pummeller realizes what the readers of classified ads have known for a very long time: a massage parlour is a knocking shop.

Fifty per cent of my friends live in respectable suburbs, but the other one lives opposite a massage parlour. She tells me that on sultry summer evenings she likes to settle herself on her balcony to watch the world. A man goes by. Then he goes by again. When going by for the third time he looks furtively over his shoulder and approaches the parlour door. From aloft my friend shouts 'Oi!'. The effect, she tells me, is gratifying.

She also tells me that a statistically improbable number of cars parked on her street contain dogs. These belong, she presumes, to suburban adventurers who have risen from the sofa, yawned, stretched and casually announced that they are just going to take the dog for a walk and they may be some time.

This explains, of course, how Captain Oates got his name, but it doesn't explain why the English-speaking peoples do these things so badly. In France they let the dogs in.

I went to a brothel once. In Acapulco. It was Peachy's idea. Peachy was a Canadian who had latched on to me in a bar and who was so driven by hormones he could have swum for China. When he found that I spoke a smattering of Spanish he begged me to take him whoring.

Perhaps it was the mescal but soon I found myself in the front seat of a taxi. Peachy sat calmly in the back trying not to drown in his own saliva.

'Where to?' snapped the driver.

I flicked a nervous hand. 'Up there,' I said.

We drove up there. 'Now where to?'

'Go on,' gurgled Peachy, 'ask him.'

I breathed in deeply. 'Well,' I said, 'my friend was wondering whether perhaps you knew of any houses of ill repute.'

The taxi-driver stopped the car. I reached for the door-handle. The driver seized my arm. I turned to him in horror. He beamed at me and rattled off an enthusiastic catalogue of the delights of seven separate establishments.

At the wrought-iron gates of La Casa Quinta a uniformed commissionaire opened the taxi door, bowed and ushered us on to a veranda. It throbbed with cheerful people. Being a virile Anglo-Saxon I scuttled to the bar. I felt acutely awkward. Already a tall woman wearing five square inches of imitation leopard-skin was feeding Peachy grapes. Peachy was gurgling dangerously.

Meanwhile back in the Bennett psyche a mass of prudish, puritan, Anglo-Saxon neuroses were shouting at me that I was out of my depth and urging me to leave. They grew too loud to ignore. Tensing my shoulders to ward off the knives that pimps were sure to try to plunge between them, I left. Out in the courtyard the commissionaire bore down on me. He bowed, opened a taxi door and apologized profusely for my disappointment. Could he, he asked, recommend the Casa Girasol?

And that, I'm afraid, was that. The nub of the matter is that La Casa Quinta was civilized and I wasn't.

And now I have a little question. Given that prostitution has been a part of every civilized society since Noah was a sailor and that every New Zealand city already abounds in bawdy houses, is it unthinkable that we should grow up and admit it? Is it unthinkable that one day I should walk down a street in this country and behold against the sky a dirty great honest neon sign saying 'Brothel'?

It is? I thought as much. I was just asking. Forget I said it. I think I'll take the dogs for a walk.

The dinky green box

The council has given most of us a dinky green box. It is meant to prick our conscience. It is meant to make us recycle. It is a dinky green box of good intentions. But as a wiser man than I has pointed out, the road to hell is paved with dinky green boxes.

You hold a party. You wake up. You stumble through the house. It resembles the Somme in 1919. The air is rich with last night. A black leopard has sunk its claws into your skull. The chaos appals you. The carpet squelches. It reflects your soul. You feel soiled and guilty and sick.

Frantic to clean your conscience you clean the house. Into a rubbish bag goes everything. Everything. Cans by the zillion, most of them skulking behind sofas. When you bend to pick them up your brain screams, but you are driven by an urge to purge. Half-drunk bottles of cheap Riesling in which cigarettes float like dead fish; whole ashtrays; shattered furniture; sleeping guests; guacamole chip dip which looks like the roof of your mouth. You try to tip it out of its bowl. It clings. You throw the whole bowl away.

You open the curtains and recoil from the sunlight like one of those fish that lives at 600 fathoms. You fling wide the windows to let today in. Deep in the bowels of your house you hear corpses stir, groan and murmur of coffee. You want them gone.

The rubbish bag in your hands threatens to burst. You carry it like guilt down the drive. By chance it is the day of the bin-man's visit. The huge sin-gobbling van is rumbling down the street. Like a priest the bin-man appears before you.

'Here,' you say, handing over your sack, 'take my guilt. O shrive me, Mr Bin-man, for I have sinned.'

He grins and shoulders your dreadful burden. Just as relief begins to flood your heart, the bag clinks. 'Hallo,' says the bin-man, the grin melting from his face, 'and what have we got here? Bottles?'

'And cans and guests and guacamole and those dreadful things I've just remembered saying to Samantha and all . . .'

But the bin-man stops you. Like the Ancient Mariner he clutches your arm and points a skinny finger. You follow with your eyes. All along your street stands a line of dinky green boxes. Each is full of flattened cans, neatly bundled newspapers, strange strings of milk cartons, and, the horror of it, washed bottles.

With a stab of something nasty you realize that you too have got one of these dinky green boxes. You used it last night to cool beer.

The bin-man priest hands you back your guilt. 'Get washing,' he says with the smug sternness of a man who holds the moral power. 'And don't let me catch you again. Or else.' And off he goes, leaving you forlorn at your gate clutching a bag of impossibility. The leopard buries its claws an inch deeper.

You do the decent thing. With the rubbish bag in the boot you drive two blocks, find a house with the curtains drawn and dump your sack of shame outside it.

But you know as you power away that the world has changed. You will hold no more parties. The generosity of your soul will shrivel. No one could wash that many bottles.

Instead, thanks to the council folly, the worst part of your nature will rise. You will join a class of person that is now spreading like meningitis through the city.

You've seen them in your own street. On bin-day they take the dog for a longer walk than usual, or they choose to go to the mall on foot. And as they go they take in the details of every dinky green box. These are the new voyeurs, the peeping toms of refuse.

For that d.g.b. lying open for inspection at every gate is nothing less than a seedy autobiography of its owner.

One glimpse of a green-label milk carton and you know that the woman in No. 7 thinks she's fat.

The old lady beyond dotes on her cat. But nestled beside those empty cans of fancy salmon dinner are the soup-for-one and baked bean tins that sing of a self-esteem which has sunk below the x-axis.

See how the dapper gentleman at No. 21 has folded the top newspaper in his bundle to expose a completed cryptic crossword.

But above all it is the bottles that count. I know a woman who smashes her gin bottles, wraps the shards in newspaper, sellotapes the package into silence and buries it deep in her rubbish bag. For her, every bin-day is a day of shame.

Furthermore the d.g.b.s have fostered malice. The woman next door irks you. She has complained to the council about your motorbike, your music, the parties you are not going to have any more. What could be easier than casually dumping an empty flagon of extremely cheap sherry in her d.g.b.? As you pass it later in the day you stop, shake your head and tut-tut loudly enough to alert the neighbours.

The council means well, but they do not understand. All unwitting they have flooded the city with vanity, meanness, prurience, malice and guilt. Take back, O Council, those dinky green boxes. Let us live.

Do it yourself

Gone are the days of getting a man in. These are the days of doing it yourself.

My neighbour, for example, a merry fellow with a two-acre toolshed, has built his own home, a modest three-storey number with a cantilevered kitchen and a solar-powered gazebo.

Faced as I was with a minor plumbing problem involving the drying up of every tap in the house, I consulted the neighbour for a noggin of free advice. After a quick prance through the airy spaces of my roof he diagnosed a case of slumped bracing in the header-tank platform and confirmed my suspicion of a frozen gland-nut on the ball-cock spindle. Both, he added, would be a breeze to fix. The word he actually used was 'fun'. He offered to help me. I laughed my do-it-yourselfer laugh, making it quite clear that there was no way he was going to muscle in on the fun in my roof, and asked if I could borrow his trailer.

His trailer had something wrong with the axle. It bounced along cheerfully on the open road, but when the builder's merchant yard called for a spot of reversing, the design fault showed up. When I turned the wheel right, the trailer went left. I explained the problem to the salesman, who told me that he had met this trailer before. With great good humour and no little skill he evicted me from the driver's seat, loaded up the trailer, charged me considerably less than my mortgage for some lovely pieces of wood and a gland-nut kit, and subjected me to the sort of gentle mockery that denotes friendship among hard practical men. Typical of his salty humour was the way he offered me the telephone number of a plumber.

Ho ho, I chuckled, and riposted with a little sally about his shorts. He took this less well than I had expected.

The lovely thing about working bent double under roofing iron at midday in summer is the climate. As I calmly measured, sawed and nailed my new bracing a family of salamanders gathered to watch and advised me to take it easy. I sneered at them and within a mere three hours I had cut two pieces of bracing, secured them with a few dozen bent nails, eaten a bushel of cobwebs, and lost twelve kilograms and a claw hammer which had slipped out of my hand on the backswing and hidden in the insulation.

After pausing to lunch on an egg which I fried on the top of my head I seized the adjustable spanner and waged war on the gland-nut. It adopted the tactic of passive resistance but I was in no mood to be thwarted. With a grunt that drew applause from the salamanders I managed finally to loosen it. Satisfaction washed over me. So did plenty of water

118

at mains pressure. It cooled the skin agreeably, then set about flooding the kitchen below.

It was the neighbour who eventually located the mains tap in the garden. It was also the neighbour who pulled out my header-tank bracing, replaced it with something admittedly a little sturdier but of less aesthetic appeal, and repacked the gland-nut.

He then gave me the phone number of a painter who would happily repaint the kitchen ceiling. The man needed work, he said. Of course, I would do it myself, but I have a generous heart.

The end of the road

I don't know how it happened. I did not see it coming. Life has snuck up behind me and stuck me between the ribs. I see little point in going on.

As a rule I expect the worst. If a friend is late for a meeting I immediately imagine that he or she is bleeding to death in a ditch. If one of my dogs doesn't emerge from the bush to my whistle I know instantly that it has been shot.

The truth, of course, turns out to be mundane. The friend arrives, the dog lollops out of the bush and life resumes its placid course.

But although I imagine the worst for other people I do not imagine the worst for myself, for the obvious reason that the worst cannot happen to me.

The Greeks had a word for this. That word was hubris. It is defined as the pride that the gods will punish. For someone stuffed with hubris, one moment all is fine and dandy, the dogs are lolloping, the sun is shining, God's in his heaven, all's right with the world, then wallop. Down comes the thunderbolt and all is sorrow. Just like that. Unpredicted and unpredictable. The nightmare that was so bad that you couldn't even dream it, becomes horrendous reality. And that is just what has happened to me. I have taken up golf.

I know, I know, you think I lie. Golf. It defies belief. Golf. Even its name sounds like a Scottish skin disease. Celtic dandruff as sport. There is nothing to be said for it. Mark Twain called it a good walk spoiled. He didn't know the half of it.

Nothing in life so confirms my fear that I have reached middle age. I had always felt somehow that I was young, that I stood, as it were, on the first tee of life, shielding my eyes against the low sun of dawn and gazing over the glistening fairways of a world made fresh with promise. But now I know that the shadows are lengthening and I am only a chip and a putt from life's eighteenth hole and the eternal clubhouse. I cannot explain how it happened. One moment of inattention and it was all over, a life in ruins.

All sport is absurd, but golf is monstrously absurd. The ball is so tiny, the course so vast and the purpose so ridiculous. God must giggle. Now he is giggling at me.

Everything about golf is wrong. President Clinton plays it. The language is wrong. I am expected to talk of birdies and bogeys without throwing up over my golf shoes with their dinky little tassles. The scoring system is wrong. A six-inch putt is worth the same as a 250-yard drive. Putting is wrong. I can't putt. I regularly putt into bunkers. I don't care. I don't want to be able to putt. Putting is for people who know their cholesterol levels.

And, oh, the unspeakability of golfers. Men with

fake Fair Isle sweaters, fake Rolex watches and genuine prostate problems, their bodies ruined by the excesses of what they like to think of as success, towing several thousand dollars' worth of titanium clubbery around in a little invalid's trolley, waddling, wobbling their buttocks and grunting, hating every minute of it but persevering because golf is the thing to do, don't you know, so suitable for someone who has made his way in the world, hacking, cursing, cheating, wheezing, then scuttling into their spiritual home the oh-so-wittily-named nineteenth where they settle round a fat glass of gin and cut deals and tell lies and burst a few more nasal capillaries. And I am now of their number. No, it's unthinkable.

Worse still are the weasel golfers, scrawny descendants of the thieving Picts who invented the game. The weasels have eyes like razor-blades, they know the rules and they always win. Down the middle of the fairway they play their conservative little shots, every club producing an identical risk-free Presbyterian hippety-hop a hundred yards down the dead dull middle of the fairway. Not for them the expansive swing, the royal drive that roars and soars and takes the world at a venture. Oh no, moderation in all things, caution is the key, know your limits, play it safe and sink the putt.

Golfers are wrong. Golf's wrong. I'm wrong. Everything's wrong. But yesterday, on the third at Charteris Bay, I swung a four-iron. It was my twenty-fifth shot of the day. But this time I did not hook and neither did I slice. No turf flew. No curses flew. The ball soared like a lark, a thing of beauty and a joy for ever, and straight as destiny it flew across a duck-egg sky and with my heart swelling like a football I watched it come to earth as gently as a kiss two paces from the hole. And, heaven help me, I was happy. There is no hope. Shoot me.

Spading the dog

If you get a puppy for Christmas, name it. But remember that the name you choose must be suitable for repeated shouting in a park. Darling is a poor choice. Châteauneuf du Pape is a poor choice. Help is a seriously poor choice.

Diet is important. Cheap dog food can stunt a puppy's growth so it is essential to buy in a stock of only the best quality shoes and furniture. Do not, however, give a puppy bones; while it is growing and its teeth are scalpel-sharp, it needs only your fingers.

Every dog has its own dietary idiosyncrasies. My first dog ate wallets. It could nose out a good leather wallet at twenty paces, and then chew through a wad of credit cards faster than a girlfriend.

As a responsible citizen you must neuter your dog. There are several technical medical terms used to describe the operation of neutering. An acquaintance once told me he had had his dog spaded. This may explain why he called the beast Doug.

Do not fret that neutering will damage your dog

psychologically. No dog ever believes it has been neutered and it will still pick out the best-dressed at a dinner party and produce moments of exquisite embarrassment.

Your dog needs to learn the habit of obeying you, and you can't start too young. The first thing that you should teach your puppy is to lay its head on your leg and dribble. To do this you need to eat an item of dog food; for example, your breakfast.

The dribble mastered, you should then teach your puppy to sit. Offer it a biscuit while leaning your weight on its haunches. As you do so, say 'sit' in a tone that means business. The dog will detect the note of seriousness and rapidly learn to leap and grab the biscuit.

Other simple commands that should be instilled in the first few months are 'stay', 'come' and 'heel'. All of these will make your puppy run away. If you wish the puppy to come back, eat breakfast.

A common error among first-time owners is to use the command 'drop'. Research has revealed that to the canine ear this command is indistinguishable from 'tug-of-war'.

As a responsible dog-owner you must scoop poops. To do this you need a plastic supermarket bag and a pound of sausages. When your dog fouls the pavement and a sour-faced woman is staring at you, bend down reasonably near to the point in question and slip the sausages into the bag. Smile at Sour Face, tie the bag of sausages, slap it about a bit, weigh it in your palm, then sling it jauntily over your shoulder. At the end of the walk use the sausages to lure the dog back. Try not to be seen feeding the dog from the pooper-scooper.

Ogden Nash defined a door as a thing that a dog is always on the other side of. To solve the door problem, remove all doors in your house. Alternatively you can install a dog-door. These come in two sizes: small burglar and fat burglar.

Owning a dog nevertheless frees you from all fear of burglary. A domestic dog will deter any burglar by a ferocious bout of licking before helping to carry the video to the getaway car. When a policeman comes to investigate the crime the dog will apologize by biting the policeman. If you want a guard dog, get a goose.

As a first-time dog-owner you will have to learn the skill of spending a lot of money on the dog. The vet will show you how. You must also learn to deal with feelings of guilt every time you leave the house, for, as Kipling warned:

Brothers and sisters, I bid you beware
Of giving your heart to a dog to tear.

The solution to the guilt problem is not to leave the house. This will save you a lot of money, which you can then give to the vet.

Two dogs are better than one because you can always disclaim ownership of fifty per cent of them.

For example, if the World Daffodil Show is being held in a marquee on Hagley Park, one of your dogs will chase a duck which will fly over the marquee. Your dog will run through the marquee. When it emerges it will be pursued by a stout woman in tweed. She will catch sight of you swinging a dog lead, and look daggers. You look innocence. You just summon your other dog and walk in the opposite direction. Your first dog will find you eventually.

(If Mrs Stout-and-Tweed is reading this, I would like to reassure her that I know a thing or two about daffs, and when I finally wrestled the bloom from the dog, it didn't look like a prize-winner to me.)

Finally, your dog will love you and it will want to sleep with you. If the dog gets on to your bed it will curl beside you with its paws by your nose and every night you will fall asleep to the fragrance of crushed grass. Throughout the night it will twitch and whimper as it chases rabbits down the long paddocks of its dreams, and every morning it will wake you with a soft paw to the jaw. This, of course, will never do. The correct way to teach your dog not to climb on to your bed is to sleep on the floor.

Happy Christmas.

Englishness abroad

Eleven years and eleven months ago I emigrated to New Zealand. Before I came people told me many things about this country. I was told that New Zealand resembled England in the fifties. Having been born in 1957 my memories of the fifties are hazy but I have a mental picture of a black-and-white decade which then became the sixties and discovered colour. I was told that Christchurch was more English than England. I was told that milk was free, and that in every hotel room they placed a jug of milk beside the bed. And New Zealand House told me that there were forty sheep for every man, woman and child in the country.

When my plane landed at Auckland I was understandably keen to meet my sheep, but we were told to stay in our seats. A little man wearing shorts and a mask then walked up the aisle spraying us with a brace of aerosols. I thought it was a hijack.

Inside the airport the security men also wore shorts. I knew at once I did not want to be arrested in this country. I would giggle.

At the immigration desk I met the local passion for forms in triplicate, but in time I was released on to the land. There, in the unlovely world of Auckland airport, I met heat, light and cabbage trees. On the walk between the terminals at Auckland the heat hummed from the concrete, the light seared and bounced, and I thought the cabbage trees were palms. This was not England in the fifties. I had rarely felt so abroad.

At the domestic terminal I ordered a coffee. The girl tipped half a teaspoon of powder into a smoked-glass mug and filled it with hot water from a boiler that could have powered the Titanic. The food cringed in scratched perspex boxes with tongs on top: thin white sandwiches under damp towels; sad asparagus rolls like Martian dog penises; and, in a pie-warmer that burned me, unsavoury savouries.

I was met at Christchurch airport by the same heat, the same light, more cabbage trees and my new headmaster. He drove me down Memorial Avenue with awesome slowness. It was midday on a Saturday. What few other cars there were, we overtook.

The road was wide, the people absent, the houses low, the sections large and sprinklers made rainbows on every lawn. I had seen something like this before, but never in England. It reminded me of Victoria in British Columbia, a place which also claimed to be more English than England. Victoria was as English as a rodeo.

I was given lunch in a garden which ran down to the Avon. What appeared to be trout nosed in the shallows. My host confirmed that they were trout.

As a boy I caught one trout. It weighed two and a half pounds. My brother suggested we should have it stuffed and mounted, but since I had poached it we ate it instead. Nevertheless, many a trout fisherman fishes a lifetime in England and never catches so large a wild trout.

Every trout in the Avon was at least the size of my monster. I asked my host if people fished for them. He said that only kids fished the Avon, and besides, these trout were 'tiddlers'.

After lunch Kate and Willy, my host's children, led me downtown. The footpaths were as hot as the sands of a desert and just as crowded. It was only years later that I heard of the man who came to New Zealand and found it shut.

I looked down Colombo Street and saw it blocked by a hill burnt brown. We climbed the cathedral spire and saw the crisp white edge of the Pacific and the crisp white tops of the Alps. Christchurch seemed a city in a cradle.

I asked the only person in the square, a woman in a heavy coat and hat, if there was anywhere nearby that I could buy food. After long thought she directed us to Johnson's Grocery. As I thanked her and turned away she told me it would be shut.

I could go on, but I am trying to take stock. All this, as I say, was eleven years and eleven months ago. Much has happened since then. The heavy hand of the weekend presses more lightly on the city now. Fewer trout swim the Avon. You can eat outdoors and the food has improved. The cars have improved and proliferated. The coffee has improved beyond measure. And we now have only twenty sheep each.

The Alps still stand, the Pacific still rolls, Willy's a builder, Kate's a policewoman and we're all eleven years older.

The abominable batsman

Cricket is a game of self-delusion. Because it calls for the skill of standing around in a paddock, many of us imagine we can still play it years beyond our use-by dates. And thus it was that across Christchurch last Sunday morning, eleven senior athletes rose while sluggard souls were still abed; we shook our lissome limbs, chewed our breakfast aspirins, packed our bags and headed forth to do battle.

The team comprised two accountants, an investment adviser, one GP, one who worked in advertising but who was nevertheless a good chap, three dentists, one columnist and two real cricketers who were there to make up the numbers and win the match.

Out of Christchurch we sped, each of us dreaming of the great things that our minds urged us to do and which our bodies defied us to try. Over the Waimak, swollen with the rains, then out across the Canterbury plain, along lethally straight roads, between windbreaks like green walls, between brown paddocks of grey sheep and on towards the purple hills of beyond and our destination, a little rural settlement which for obvious legal reasons I shall not name.

The domain at Cust is a sweet place. The rain, however, had turned the pitch to suet. The three wise dentists prodded it with thumbs and keys and muttered dark technical terms like hangover. Of the three dentists, one was skinny, the second wasn't. Nor, indeed, was the third, but since he sometimes gets to tut over my teeth, I shall call him merely Grandpa Dentist. All three of them, of course, displayed the enviable muscle-tone that comes from humping heavy wallets to the bank.

Already the nor'wester was bending the macrocarpas and the sky held that pure deep blue found only above the plains of Canterbury. The pitch would dry rapidly.

By winning the toss the investment adviser proved he had mastered the only skill that his profession requires. He invited Cust to bat. In the tiny dressing room we warmed up by wrestling with trousers that had once fitted. The senior accountant, a key figure in our bowling attack, pulled on a shirt which announced that he had taken part in a Golden Oldies tournament in 1979.

On to the field we ran to the wild applause of a paddockful of hoggets. While the GP paced out his run from the bottom end, nine fielders gathered at first slip. It took stern captaincy from the investment adviser to distribute them about the field like a sound portfolio. As was fitting, Grandpa Dentist remained at first and second slip.

Enter, with heavy tread, the wild man of Cust, the abominable batsman. Huge he was, his bat a matchstick in his giant paw. He wore one pad, one glove and big black boots. On the face of his bat were drawings of three skulls, and above them the word 'Smashed'.

The GP bowled, the wild man swung and the hoggets scattered. The advertising man bowled and the wild man swung and Dentist One trotted off into the stand of pinus radiata. The numbers on the scoreboard whirred.

But then in the third over the wild man swung and the ball went up and the ball kept on going up and then it started to come down and underneath it stood Captain Investment, eyes trained on its descent as if it were a falling Dow.

It was pleasant to sit in little groups on the grass and natter of this and that while the investment adviser toddled off to the pavilion to have his finger bandaged, but eventually he returned, the wild man was bowled by one of the real cricketers and play became more sedate. At lunch the game was as evenly balanced as the plateful of pies which Grandpa Dentist dispatched in the garden behind the Cust Hotel.

One of the real cricketers opened our innings and bludgeoned the bowling, while the junior accountant collected runs with the exuberance typical of his profession. Local rules required the real cricketer to retire at forty, and thereafter wickets fell. A good catch ruled off the accountant's ledger and Dentist Two studiously left a wide ball which flattened his leg-stump. But everyone got a few and with Dentist One prodding and probing and occasionally drilling the half-volley the game neared its climax. With two runs still needed Dentist One reached the total of compulsory retirement and Grandpa Dentist strode to the middle, pausing only twice on the trek to regain his breath. Only the senior accountant was left to come in. Tension crackled.

The GP flailed his bat and the ball scudded past the fielder but stopped short of the boundary. 'Yes,' shouted the GP, 'two there!' and Grandpa Dentist set off on a forty-four-yard odyssey that would end in glory or an ambulance. Glory won by a short head and while we whooped and hollered the GP gently defibrillated Grandpa Dentist with a can of DB.

All that remained was to fling a few hoggets on the barbecue and to start telling lies. By the time we drove home, our rear-view mirrors golden with the light of the setting sun, we believed them.

Finns and photos

The camera is responsible for most of the ills of the late twentieth century. It has brought us *One Network News*. It has brought us supermodels with the legs of wading birds and brains to match. Above all it has turned travel into tourism.

I have a dream, a dream of revolution. Even little men can dream.

The revolution begins on a bench in the Botanical Gardens with a loaf of bread, a mob of ducks and four Finnish tourists. I can tell they are tourists because they are dressed in identical cameras. I can tell they are Finns because they pronounce their *o*'s with a line through them.

The leader of the Finns, a sour and burly fellow by the name of Dorsal, barks at his companions.

'Go and stand by the man who is the ducks feeding,' he barks.

His three companions sulk across to my bench and pose.

'For the love of Ødin,' bellows Dorsal as he points his camera, 'smile!'

They try to smile. It is a sorry sight.

'Helsinki,' I say.

'Helsinki,' they reply, in evident astonishment at the fluency of my Finnish.

'Permit me the photograph for you to take,' I say, putting a careful line through each of my *o*'s. I arrange the gloomy Finn foursome in a tableau beside the bench and tell them to shut their eyes and count to a hundred. As they stand in blind bafflement I sprint for the Avon and hurl the Pentax into the water where it is snaffled by a handsome trout.

Panting Finns chase me, encircle me and bristle.

'Helsinki,' I say, stalling. They are not to be put off. But nor am I.

From Dorsal's neck I snatch a self-loading, auto-focus C129 Canon and swing it around my head by its imitation leather strap with the practised ease of the professional lassooist I used to be. 'Tourists of the world, unite,' I bellow, first in Finnish and then in eleven other languages as a guided party emerges from the rose garden and gathers to watch, 'You have nothing to lose but your chains.' And so saying I fling the Canon in a soaring parabola out over the glistening water to a collective polylingual gasp of delighted horror from the crowd of several hundred. The camera catches the sunlight like a camera catching sunlight and then sinks to the waiting trout. The tourists stand aghast.

'Have you,' I boom as I pluck a Ricoh from a Japanese hand, 'have you, Hiroshi, no idea of the tyranny of film? Can you not see that every photograph is false, that the camera always lies, that you take photos only to convince yourself that

you have had a good' – and here the Ricoh flies –
'time?'

I seize a Handycam.

'Yea, verily, I say unto you,' I say unto them
verily, 'the camera is the devil.'

The Handycam takes wing.

'All those shots of the Church of the Good
Shepherd at Tekapo, of Timaru shopping centre, of
what might be Mount Cook from the bus window,
they are a substitute for living. You are so busy
taking photographs you are forgetting to be. Buy
yourself a dozen postcards, throw away your
cameras and live!' To underline the point I toss an
SLR into Davy Jones's locker. 'Thank you,' says
Davy.

By now the crowd has swelled to several hundred
thousand tourists, every one of them agog. 'Ladies
and gentlemen,' I go on in fluent Gog, 'take pity at
least on your neighbours. Do you imagine they
want to see your holiday snaps? Do you imagine
that you do not make them groan with dread? Do
you imagine that they have the least interest in a
shot of Hiroshi or Klaus or Dorsal' – and here I
throw a manly arm around a Finnish shoulder –
'grinning by the Hokitika Civic Fountain? Do you?
Well do you?'

This is the critical moment. The crowd vacillates.
Suddenly my old friend Dorsal seizes the initiative
and with a single fluid movement tosses it into the
water. The crowd roars as one and the sky grows
dark with cameras flung. Kodaks and Leicas by the
tens of thousands arc through the bright air and the

138

tourists whoop and dance. They are free.

It is a far far better thing that I have done than I have ever done before. I return smug to the ducks, then to the Dux. Even little men can dream.

Principal principles

In the bad old days it took two people to run a school, the principal and the deputy principal. They were the yin and yang of education. Principals were dreamers. They saw their schools as ideal states. Deputy principals, on the other hand, were realists. They saw schools as battlezones. Old-fashioned deputy principals frightened children into obedience. If this failed they hit the children with implements.

In the old days the position of deputy principal was advertised thus: 'Wanted: Deputy Principal. Must have gimlet eyes, small moustache and private armoury. The position is open to both men and women. Send photograph of armoury.'

But the bad old days are over. I have in front of me an advertisement for a deputy principal for a school in Christchurch. The school has employed a 'consulting group' to write the ad for them and I would like to thank the school for doing so, since it has produced a spectacular piece of consultant-speak.

The ad starts quietly by stating that the deputy principal will be 'a key member of the management teams'. Even though this phrase appears to say something, an alert nostril will sniff the approach of piffle. The phrase suggests that the deputy principal will help to run the school. Such information will hardly come as a surprise to applicants. Notice also the magnificent use of the word 'key'. It means nothing.

The author then revs up: '. . . the appointee will facilitate the ongoing development of the school's future positioning, strategic, quality management and planning processes . . .' Every budding consultant should study this extract. Its only fault is that it contains the concrete noun 'school'. This should be replaced with 'educational environment'. Otherwise it's perfect. In addition to the vacuous nouns, the author has made use of 'ongoing', an adjective so empty it can, and should, be slotted in anywhere.

'Facilitate' is in vogue. According to the dictionary, it means to make easy, but from my experience of 'facilitators' it means the opposite. Such ambiguity brings joy to a consultant's heart.

In the old days when the art teacher arrived at school late, dishevelled and smelling like a goat, it was the deputy principal who took him aside and barked at him. The modern DP, however, will do nothing so drastic. Instead he or she 'will manage the effective operation of the performance management and development systems'. I suspect performance management still means barking at smelly art teachers, but one has to admire the verbal mush. I particularly like the idea of managing the operation of management. A word to note here is 'effective' which can be used in the same way as ongoing. The only difference is that effective does mean something. It means ineffective.

It takes an exceptional person to manage the operation of management, and the ad spells out just how exceptional. 'The position requires proven leadership and management skills, complemented by sound administrative and interpersonal capabilities.'

As a rule, any writing that uses the word 'skills' is claptrap, but here we see claptrap *in excelsis*. The phrase 'interpersonal capabilities' is the work of a maestro.

Nevertheless, the author has yet to climax. Cop this one. 'Central to this role is the customer service interface, both internal and external.' Years ago and in a foreign country I knew a divinity teacher who was fond of internal customer service interfacing. Then one of the customers told his mum.

I have attacked consultant-speak before. When I did so, one consultant wrote to tell me that I was unfair. Not all consultants wrote rubbish, he told me, and I hope he is right. Nevertheless, lots of them do write rubbish and I am mocking their language again because it needs to be mocked. Bad language is dangerous.

We live in a world of things and deeds. Language names those things and deeds and enables us to consider them, to order them and to understand them. It is our best tool for thinking. In short, language civilizes us.

If we use language badly we think less clearly and

we become less civilized. The advertisement for the deputy principal is a wicked thing because it is most likely to attract applicants who use similar language. Since applicants must apply in the first instance to the consulting group rather than to the school, I fear for the chances of any aspiring deputy principal who writes a blunt and honest application.

To become a deputy principal is to set foot on the ladder of educational promotion. On higher rungs stand principals and school inspectors (who are now called something else) and higher still stand policy-makers. If blather can get you on the ladder, then it can also push you up it. If you do not believe me, read anything that emerges from the ministry of Education or the NZQA*.

Language is what distinguishes us from the beasts of the field and the fowls of the air. The advertisement I have quoted from makes as much sense as the quacking of ducks. I am fond of ducks, but I do not want them in charge of education.

---

*The New Zealand Qualifications Authority, the governmental body charged with the annual task of making exams easier.

Let the togas fall

Accidents happen, thank God. I had one last night. It involved Kerry, Lindsey, Maddie, Marcus and rather a lot of bottles. Kerry, Lindsey, Maddie and Marcus have gone, I think, but the bottles have stayed. They stand about me now in silent witness. From the evidence it seems we may also have eaten something. I wonder what it was.

Parties come in two varieties: good parties and excellent parties. It is possible to plan a good party but the excellent ones, like last night's, are accidents. Accidental parties hum because a party is a return to a state of nature. It is raw and random life. It is hard to plan for raw and random.

Nice people need parties. This is because nice people are not entirely nice. In order to live in an orderly and artificial society we have to lie a lot. We say good morning when we don't mean it. We ask how people are when we don't want to know. We restrain our urges to do unspeakable things.

At parties we don't. We say what we mean and we do what we want. It's a psychological pressure valve and a very good thing.

All societies have held parties. Once a year that

most orderly race, the Romans, took a week off from road-building to have a belter of a bash. They called it the Saturnalia. The essence of it was to invert the normal world. Work stopped, wine flowed and togas fell. Slaves bullied masters, judges frolicked with waitresses and into the woods they all wandered to have a very good time indeed. The ground was littered with discarded inhibitions.

To hold a party you need three things: somewhere to have it, someone to have it with and lots of booze.

Cram ten people into a phone-box and they start laughing. The same holds true of parties. Keep the space small. All parties should be held in someone else's house, but if an accident occurs and you become the host, make part of your house out of bounds – the indoors part, for example.

Let chance choose your guests. An effective way to do this is to open your door and play music. Serendipity will deliver you just the right people. You should have a sprinkling of lechers, a few depressives who'll sit on the stairs and talk wrists, and at least one person who can't sing and wants to.

As spices are to a stew, so gatecrashers are to a party. Let them in. Don't worry about damage. Your friends will do that. Do bar the door, however, to men with cheap wine. Send them away to buy the beer they are going to want to drink.

Once the ingredients are assembled, a party just happens. It is unwise, and often dangerous, to try to direct it.

I neglected to mention that the Roman Saturnalia

took place at the end of December. The Romans felt the need to clear out the old year with the chaos of honest debauch. Out of that fertile soil the next orderly year could grow strong.

So, if you woke this morning to stabs of guilt, if your tongue looks and tastes like a slug, if your brain thuds and your bones ache and you can think of several people whom you could not look in the eye, then you have done your bit to maintain a long, healthy and deeply human tradition. Happy New Year.

Death by accident insurance

Because I have a gift for locking my keys in my car I pay an annual subscription to an association which knows how to break into cars.

This association has just sent me an envelope with the words 'How often does someone offer you something for nothing?' on the front. Beside these words stands a cartoon character called Doubting Thomas.

Of course, Doubting Thomas was the apostle who refused to believe that Christ had risen 'unless I . . . put my finger into the print of the nails and thrust my hand into his side'. Christ invited him to finger and thrust as much as he wished whereupon Doubting Thomas stopped doubting and went to wash his hands.

What the motoring association wishes to offer me for nothing is 'a gift of free accidental death insurance, provided free of charge . . .' I was thrilled to learn that the thing offered for nothing was a gift, and that not only was it a gift but it was also free, and furthermore it was free of charge. I know I tend to leap to conclusions, but I must admit to gaining the impression that I wouldn't have to pay anything.

What they are offering is $2,000 worth of 'free death by accident insurance'. A hyphen or two would have helped here. Free death does not attract me. It is already available. Furthermore, death by accident insurance sounds nasty. I picture accountants with bad breath reading me policy statements until I peg out.

What they mean, of course, is that if I take up the offer and then cark it in a car crash they will pay $2,000 to my dogs. As it happens, my dogs are already well provided for, but the motoring chaps would have had no way of knowing this – unless of course they asked Inland Revenue, who for $20 will apparently tell anyone my address, sexual preference and inside-leg measurement (which, as chance would have it, is also my sexual preference).

But why should my motoring pals want to give me insurance? Well, let them speak for themselves. 'The free cover is our way of saying thank you for being a loyal . . . member.' Well, that's what I call a really touching little lie.

I have not been loyal. The association provides a service which I choose to buy. If I found a way of not locking my keys in the car, I would stop paying them money. Loyalty does not come into it. They are flattering me.

They are also luring me. They want me to buy more insurance. The letter goes on to tell me that for a mere $13 a month I could net my dogs $100,000 simply by doing a spot of accidental dying. $100,000 is a lot of dog roll.

To encourage me to buy that insurance they try

to frighten me with statistics. They also scatter more cartoons of Doubting Thomas. In the first cartoon he is 'slightly tempted'. In the next he is 'definitely wavering'. In the last triumphant frame he has 'no doubts'. Doubting T. will fill in his acceptance form straight away.

This letter encapsulates the late twentieth century. It tries to sell me something. It baits me. It tells fibs. It trivializes history. And it is written in shoddy English. I shall burn it.

And if the motoring association sends me any more biblical nonsense to try to sell me insurance I shall direct them to the last eight words of Ecclesiastes 9:11.

Tat

Poor Mr Lee Williams. Mr Williams is twenty-three years old and he lives in America. America is a nice place and Mr Williams is young so he should be happy but he is sad.

One day Mr Williams went to a place where people write on you for money and what they write doesn't come off. The place he went to was called Eternal Tattoos. Eternal means that what they write on you really seriously doesn't come off.

Lots of people have tattoos. Most of these people are boys. Some girls have got tattoos but my mum says they are not nice girls and I should not talk to them, even when they talk to me. My mum says that good girls don't have tattoos because good girls have got more sense.

Anyway, Mr Williams isn't a girl. He is a very tough man. The trouble was that lots of people didn't know how tough he was so Mr Williams wanted to get a tattoo which would tell them. Then he wouldn't have to bash them up all the time. He could just show them his tattoo and they would say, 'Ooooh you're tough, Mr Williams,' and he would say, 'Yes.'

So Mr Williams went up to the nice man in Eternal Tattoos and said, 'I would like a tattoo which tells people I am tough.' The nice man said that all tattoos told people you were tough and what tattoo did Mr Williams want. Mr Williams thought a bit and he said, 'I want you to write VILLAIN on my arm.'

'Okay,' said the tattooist.

Mr Williams was happy because he knew that the word VILLAIN would frighten people. If he went into a bank he could just roll his sleeve up and point at his tattoo and people would say, 'After you, Mr Villain,' and let him go to the front of the queue. And if he wanted to buy something in a shop he could ask the price and when the girl in the shop said a big price Mr Williams could point at his arm and say a small price and the girl would say, 'Okay.'

When Mr Williams came out with his new tattoo on his arm he was very proud. The first thing he did was to go into a clothes shop and buy a dozen T-shirts with nice short sleeves. He put one of the T-shirts on then he went up to an old lady in the street and he showed her his tattoo and said, 'Grrrr.'

The old lady opened her handbag and took out her glasses and put them on. Then she started laughing. 'Ha ha,' said the old lady.

'Grrrr,' said Mr Williams again very loudly, but the old lady laughed and laughed. 'Stop laughing,' said Mr Williams, 'I'm a VILLAIN.'

'No you're not,' said the old lady. She was wiping tears from her eyes. 'You're a VILLIAN.'

Mr Williams looked at his arm and the old lady was right. He was a VILLIAN. Mr Williams sat down in the road and started crying. 'Boo hoo,' said Mr Williams, 'I wanted to be a VILLAIN.'

'There there,' said the old lady, and she put her arm around him and gave him her hanky to blow his nose. 'Don't worry about a silly old tattoo,' she said. 'I bet you're really a very tough villain indeed.' She was a very nice old lady.

Mr Williams went back into the clothes shop with his arm behind his back and he swapped the dozen T-shirts with short sleeves for a dozen T-shirts with long sleeves and then he went home to be sad.

But the story might still have a happy ending because Mr Williams lives in America which is a place with lots of lawyers. One day a lawyer heard about the tattoo that was spelt wrong and he went to see Mr Williams. 'I am a lawyer,' said the lawyer.

'I am a villain,' said Mr Williams, carefully covering up his arm, 'I break the law.'

'Don't be silly,' said the lawyer, 'the law is your friend. We will sue the nasty tattooist.'

'Oooh, what a good idea!' said Mr Williams, and the nice lawyer wrote a letter to Eternal Tattoos and asked for $25,000. The lawyer said it was for 'distress and embarrassment'.

My mum told me to say that there is a moral to this story. She said that most tattoos are a form of infantile wish-fulfilment which gratify a desire to render a temporary condition permanent, and to turn a hope into a truth. Furthermore, said my mum, tattoos reflect a primitive voodoo faith in the potency of words and symbols. This particular story, she said, illustrates human hypocrisy, the insincerity of rebellion, the universality of greed and the absurdity of the law.

I don't understand any of that. I just feel sorry for Mr Williams. I hope he gets his money.

Things

God knows what I was thinking of, but today I bought a thing, an ornamental thing. The end can't be far away now.

Yes, I know, there's enough hell to be had with people, let alone things, what with the advertising bore and the real-estate bore and the talkback bore and the rugby mega-bore and the financial adviser whose advice ought to be to become a financial adviser because it is the only job he has ever held down and it has made him rich, but even these unspeakable people have one virtue which things don't have. Even though these people may keep me from the drinks trolley with their jokes off the internet and their slip-on shoes and their un-dissuadable self-regard, and even though they may corner me and lecture me until my brain is molten with rage, I am consoled by the knowledge that these people will be somewhere else tomorrow.

Not so with things. Things are worse than people. Things are the real enemy. Hold a good messy party and however messy the people get they will at least go away in the end and clean themselves up. Things won't. Ashtrays, bottles, plates, discarded clothing, stains and sticky furniture will wait patiently through the night to greet you in the horror morning like the claws of conscience.

The only language things understand is violence. 'Never underestimate,' says an Owen Marshall character, 'the perversity of objects', and in one of the most gratifyingly violent scenes in world literature he takes a crow-bar to a malfunctioning pump.

Don't acquire things. Things fill the house and shrivel the soul. Who amongst us has not got a cupboard of things that were thought once to bestow ease and wonder on our lives but became dump-fodder within days? Bread-makers, miniature vacuum cleaners, datadays, exercycles, solar-powered shoe trees, all of them now standing in mute testimony to our acquisitive folly, our possessive myopia, our desperate yearning for a better world.

Once upon a time we were kids at Christmas who couldn't sleep for the excitement of being given things. But then we unwrapped the things and instantly discarded the things and started looking forward to Christmas again. And we remain kids at Christmas, but nobody loves us any more so we have to buy ourselves things and it still doesn't do the trick.

The worst of the lot are ornaments. There comes a day in the offal-pit of disappointment known as middle-age, when you attend a Sunday market and in among all the tosh and garbage, the home-pickled vegetables, the unidentifiable bits of used plumbing, the cracked crockery, the *Complete Home Handyman 1971–74* bound in genuine leatherette, you find a pretty something and you finger the pretty something and the woman in the coat looks up and senses weakness and says it's rather nice, isn't it? You ho-hum noncommittally but the ghastly blank of home is shouting to you that it would look nice on the mantelpiece and it's only $9 and, well, it's just like the moment when you stop at the top of a particularly steep bit of ski-slope and you peer over.

Streams of children ski past you and over the cliff with a whoop, so finally humiliation launches you off the edge with a dread in your throat and a lump in your heart and after that it's just gravity and terror. Same with ornaments. Buy one and you're a gone possum. You've entered a world without limits, a world of china drayhorses, cats in brandy balloons, landlady paintings of lolling *señoritas* and commemorative Charles and Di plates.

I know. I've done it. The rest home looms.

Smile at the nice
axe-murderer

California has given us a new hero. Most Californian heroes are artificial and implausible media creations – Mel Gibson, Leonardo di Caprio, Ronald Reagan – but this new hero is of an earthier nature.

Her name is Richelle Roberts and she works as a produce clerk in a supermarket in Martinez, California. I presume this means she builds pyramids of tomatoes, and plasters them with those informative stickers which tell you that what you have just picked up is a tomato. And perhaps Richelle Roberts longs for Mel Gibson to wheel a trolley up her aisle so that she can slip him a pomegranate. Anyway it sounds a pleasant life.

But Richelle Roberts is unhappy, and not just because people keep asking if her name is a spelling mistake. She is unhappy because men who are not Mel Gibson keep accosting her at work. They bail her up against the apricots and tell her she's a peach.

Nor is Richelle the only one to be accosted.

Eleven other women at this supermarket share her feelings. So tired are they of hiding behind water melons to avoid the attentions of men who are not Mel Gibson that they have filed grievances against their employer, the Safeway supermarket chain.

The cause of all this unhappiness is the company's 'Superior Service' policy, according to which employees are required to 'anticipate customers' needs, take them to items they can't find, make selling suggestions, thank them by name if they pay by cheque or credit card, and offer to carry out their groceries.' Above all they must 'smile and make eye-contact'.

Thus if an axe-murderer out on parole for good behaviour asks Richelle what's hot in fresh fruit, Richelle has to gaze into his troubled eyes, smile, pack paw-paws into a bag for him and carry them out to the boot of his car. If Prince Charming then happens to bundle Richelle into the boot with the paw-paws and drive her off to the trailer park to practise his cleaver work, that, as they say, is tough bananas. While he hacks at her limbs the Superior Service policy requires Richelle to look him in the eye and ask if he is having a nice day.

What we're dealing with here, of course, is marketing. It used to be called selling. Door-to-door salesmen since time began have practised the big smile and the glad eye. It makes the customer feel liked. Being liked arouses the happiness gland and the happiness gland opens the wallet.

One of the most distinctive qualities of salesmen, however, is that most of them are men. By and large men are bigger and stronger than women. Furthermore, salesmen have always been free to smile. Richelle Roberts and her colleagues do not have that choice.

If a woman looks a man in the eye and flashes the sort of teeth that only the Americans seem to manage, a man tends to feel very good indeed. All sorts of testosteronic things surge through his veins. Too many men struggle to master testosteronic things, which is why Richelle Roberts finds herself up against the apricots more often than she would wish.

Well, Richelle Roberts has had enough. She insists that she should decide for herself 'who I am going to say hello to with a big smile'. But the management of Safeway thinks differently.

The spokeswoman for Safeway is called Debra Lambert, which confirms suspicions about Californian spelling. Ms Lambert admits that since January the company has been sending 'undercover shoppers' into its supermarkets. If Richelle and her colleagues don't smile at the secret agents they receive 'negative evaluations'. 'Negative evaluations' lead to 'remedial training'. Any failure to be remedially trained can lead to that altogether simpler thing, the sack.

Spokeswoman Lambert admits that 'sometimes customers get out of line' but she doesn't see it 'as a direct result of our initiative'. By 'initiative' Ms Lambert means the Superior Service policy.

As so often the problem lies with words. Debra Lambert is bound to be in the wrong because she can say 'negative evaluations' and 'remedial train-ing' without throwing up.

But the nub of the matter is in the word 'service'. What Safeway calls service is not service. Service is courtesy, politeness, attentiveness, thoughtfulness. It is the recognition of a relationship between seller and buyer.

Eye-contact and a flash of teeth denote a relation-ship not between seller and buyer, but between people as people. The eyes and the mouth signal personal interest. Richelle Roberts is employed to sell fruit and vegetables, but the Superior Service policy requires her to sell herself.

In short, Safeway hired a person but, in order to make more money, they wish her to become a retail whore. They wish her to use body-language to tell lies. Richelle Roberts is fighting, not for the free-dom to be discourteous or inattentive, but for the freedom to be honest, to be herself. It is a cause worth fighting for.

Lying doggo

My dog ran down the drive after a cat and hit a car. The impact bowled him twenty metres down the road. His thigh-bone was smashed to pieces.

When twenty years ago I broke my leg, there may have been a couple of Mongolian peasants who didn't hear about it but I think I let everyone else know. My screams split the sky and, in the days that followed, the fading echo of those screams was replaced by the gentle sloshing sound of a young man wallowing in self-pity.

Not so the dog. He whimpered, more it seemed from bewilderment than pain. When I reassured him he fell silent and merely trembled.

The vet doped him so strongly that the dog didn't even notice when I left him lying on a synthetic sheepskin on a floor that smelt of disinfectant. On the operating table the following morning the vet reassembled the pieces of bone and held them together with a system of metal rods and clamps, most of them sitting outside the leg. I saw the x-rays. I thought the reconstituted leg looked haphazard, too jumbled to knit into strong new bone, but I didn't say so.

The x-ray was easier to look at than the leg itself. It was shaved, angry, bloody, taut and hugely swollen. It looked like what it was, a piece of damaged meat, a condemned leg of lamb, a vast and putrid ham, a dead thing.

The dog was too weak and drugged to stand but he moaned when I left him. I drank sedatives myself that evening but slept fitfully. My mind conjured images of suffering.

I picked him up the next day. When I arrived his tail thumped the linoleum. He struggled on to three legs, leaning against a plastic cage and panting. When I went to the till to pay he whimpered and hobbled after me.

In the car-park he smelt out my car. I had a towel to wrap under his belly to lift him on to the back seat but he needed no help. Back in a familiar place he whined gently with what seemed both pleasure and pain. I wound the window down. He stuck his face into the rush of passing air in the ancient manner of dogs and fell silent.

I dreaded having to help him up the steep and sharp-edged concrete steps to my house but I need not have worried. His lust for home drove him up them in a supercanine effort, dragging his useless leg like a sack of offal. My other dog nuzzled and licked the wound. The cat cautiously toured him.

He checked the familiar details of the house and he saw that it was good and he drank a bowl of water and I swear that he sighed with relief. Then he lay down to get better.

It is now five days since I brought him home. In

162

that time he has uttered no complaint except when the cat batted a ping-pong ball around him. Even when he tried to climb on to the sofa and crumpled backwards on to the floor he merely yelped a single involuntary yelp.

The leg remains useless. Thin, bloody fluids have leaked from it and he has licked them away. He has cleaned every wound a hundred times. The plum-coloured anger has drained a little from the outside of the leg but the inside of the haunch remains as bruised as a tropical sunset. On the shaved skin a grizzle of hair has sprouted, like the first awaken-ings of a spring crop.

I am confident he will recover.

Far more significantly, so is he. In the last half hour I have battled to pin down in words what it is that I find so touching and admirable in my dog's manner. It is something to do with acceptance and faith, with trust and modesty. Patience seems to be the key word, derived from *patior* which means to suffer. I have sought the exact words but I have not found them.

And then a woman rang from Ashburton and we nattered of this and that and dogs and literature and for some reason a passage of Whitman came into my mind and it says all I want to say.

> I think I could turn and live with animals, they
>   are so placid and self-contained,
> I stand and look at them long and long.
> They do not sweat and whine about their
>   condition,

They do not lie awake in the dark and weep for
their sins,
They do not make me sick discussing their duty
to God,
Not one is dissatisfied, not one is demented with
the mania of owning things,
Not one kneels to another, nor to his kind that
lived thousands of years ago,
Not one is respectable or unhappy over the
whole earth.

Thank you Mr Rodgers

I had been thinking that management consultants did not read newspapers. I had been rude about them and not one had replied. But now Mr Murray Rodgers has stood up for his profession and I doff my hat to him.

Mr Rodgers tells me I quack like a duck, which is fair enough because I had said much the same about one of his fellow consultants. He also said I should play with my duck in the bath while the modern world passes me by. That's fair enough too. I enjoy as much as the next chap a bit of ongoing infancy simulation in a non-conflict aquatic cleansing environment, and as for what Mr Rodgers chooses to call the modern world, well I'm happy for it to trot on by as much as it wishes.

But lest we forget what we are discussing, I wrote to attack the language of an advertisement for the position of deputy principal at a local school. The job description announced that 'the appointee will facilitate the ongoing development of the school's future positioning, strategic, quality management and planning processes'. There was plenty more such guff. Mr Rodgers says that he didn't write this guff but that he could easily have done so. That's some admission.

I object to language like this because it says little, bears little relation to reality, is needlessly complex and aims to impress by that complexity. It can be boiled down to very little. For example in the passage I have quoted, the word 'ongoing' means nothing. If development doesn't go on, then it isn't development. And instead of 'facilitating development' why can't the appointee just 'develop' something? The reason, I suspect, is that it sounds less impressive.

The appointee will develop the 'school's future positioning'. Well, he or she could hardly develop its past positioning, so let's cross out the word 'future'. If positioning means what it ought to mean then it will need a big truck. I presume it does not mean that, but exactly what it does mean I cannot tell you. I wonder if the author can.

From Mr Rodgers' article I have learned that 'strategic, quality management' means ensuring that the teachers teach well and that they contribute to making the school a happy, busy and harmonious place. These are laudable aims. They are also not new aims.

Mr Rodgers tells us that 'the way people behave in organizations has changed remarkably over the last ten years'. True, they now employ consultants a lot more than they used to.

According to Mr Rodgers, the boss should 'treat staff as equals rather than as lower-class servants'. Well, over the last twenty years I have taught in several schools in several countries. All but one boss I have worked for has respected me. My bosses have asked me and my colleagues for our opinions. We have had meetings and committees. They have allowed us to work independently, and acknowledged the things we are good at, and thanked us and been open to suggestions. They have not needed a strategic plan to do this; they have needed wisdom, modesty and humanity. The best principals under whom I have worked have been outstanding people.

The implication of this is that either schools are different from business organizations – and in some important ways they are – or that Mr Rodgers' wonderful new discoveries about the way organisations work are not so new.

Mr Rodgers tells me that no longer would a deputy principal 'bark at smelly art teachers' but would tell the teacher 'what his wicked ways are . . . how to fix them and what the consequences would be of not fixing them'.

Well, I confess to exaggeration in the words 'bark' and 'smelly'. I find jokes and emphatic words irresistible. Nevertheless, had the teacher smelt and the DP barked, it would still have been clear to the smelly one what he had to do to avoid another bark, and how a bark could become a bite.

And however strategic your plans, and however developed your school's positioning might be, art teachers will still arrive at school from time to time with hangovers because they are people.

The irony of Mr Rodgers' article is that he writes clearly. For the benefit of unreconstructed dinosaurs like myself he explains 'strategic planning' and 'performance-management processes' in words that I can understand. In doing so he shows these ideas to be simple, obvious and in no way revolutionary. I cannot speak of industrial organizations because I know nothing of them, but good teachers have been running their classes in this way for years and good principals, their schools.

Furthermore Mr Rodgers apologizes for the blather. 'Our ability to match the English language to these changes in a clear and succinct way is still catching up.' This is flawed reasoning. For one thing, as I have said, Mr Rodgers manages to express himself clearly and succinctly in his article.

But more importantly he has misunderstood the relationship between language and thought. In rational matters like this, we think largely through words. It is not a question of the words catching up with the idea because, in the act of thinking, words and the idea become one. If the words are woolly it is because the thinking is shoddy.

To put it simply, Mr Rodgers says that consultants have not got the words they need to say the things they want to say. Yes, they have. As Mr Rodgers shows in his article, most things can be explained simply. And that is how they should be explained.

My beef is with the language. Let Mr Rodgers and his fellows work out what they have to say and say it as simply as possible. If they did this we would often see emperors wearing the ideal clothes for bathtime with ducks.

The man who ate death

It started with the toast. I laid before him a slice of free-range wholemeal and a sliver of fat-free spread. As I turned away to bear glasses of hot water to table 21, he called me back, indicated the fat-free spread and asked what it was. I told him. He pushed it away.

'Butter,' he said, 'bring me butter.' Just like that. The women at table 21 turned to stare but he didn't seem to care. 'And lots of it,' he added.

Well, service is my middle name. I would have preferred Gloria, but life wasn't meant to be easy.

From the boss I collected the key to the dangerous goods cupboard, fetched a pottle of butter and bore it to him at arm's length. The stench of cholesterol made me retch.

'What's that?' he asked, pointing at the side of the pottle.

'That?' I said breezily. 'Oh, nothing much. Just the mandatory health warning, you know. Butter kills.' I meant it to sting.

He ordered two more pottles. The couple at the next table left the brasserie in a huff and a hurry. Lunacy disquiets people. The man spread the butter so thickly that he left toothmarks.

The women at table 21 began to twitter as birds in the Amazon jungle twitter when they have seen a tree-snake.

The man seemed not to notice them. 'Bacon,' he said, 'bring me streaky bacon. And fried bread.'

No sooner had he spoken than a crash shook every table on the little patio as a woman slumped from her chair to the ground. Twenty hands rushed to her aid. The owners of the hands rushed after them. 'Is there a health professional in the house?' I cried but it was too late. With the words 'fried bread' on her lips, and a look on her face that will stay with me until the day I forget it, the woman went limp as old lettuce. She had sipped her last hot water.

We turned as one to stare at the man whose words had shocked a vegetarian fat-free heart into stillness.

'White bread,' he said, 'it has to be white bread. Fried in the bacon fat until it glistens to the core. Add goose fat if possible.'

Too numb to do anything else I relayed the murderer's request to the short-order chef. He blanched. He also steamed and roasted, but he did not know how to fry. I explained the process. I could see that it shocked him but in the best tradition of short-order chefs he drew himself up to his full four foot six and set to work.

Carrying the plate out to the patio I could feel myself gagging at the smell despite the mask that Occupational Safety and Health requires to be worn by all people working with fried food. Customers recoiled from me, wrinkling their noses like boxer dogs. One woman's hand slipped to her breast and clutched involuntarily at a crucifix. A stout party in a yellow trouser-suit fainted.

The monster seemed oblivious to the general horror. He calmly buttered the fried bread, heaped the bacon on top of it, showered the pile with salt, carved off a forkful, raised it to his lips and . . . I had to turn away.

'Coffee,' he bellowed at my back, 'coffee with cream.' I was glad of the chance to flee. By now, customers were scrambling for the exits but the news had spread and their way was blocked by ghouls who flocked to see the man who ate death. I battled through the horde.

He sipped the coffee and spat it. 'I want real coffee,' he barked, 'coffee with caffeine.' The crowd gasped. Several more matrons hit the deck like sacks of matrons.

I was past caring. As I made his drug-laden coffee I didn't even bother with the mask. Ambulance officers lugged out shock victim after shock victim. Television cameras arrived. A little man in big glasses offered me wads for an exclusive. I brushed him aside and took the coffee to the table. The patio looked like Passchendaele. By now the man had eaten and was reading the newspaper. He topped the coffee with cream, sipped, sighed, reached into his pocket, drew forth a cigarette and lit it. The stampede was instantaneous. In ten seconds the place was deserted but for a litter of corpses, some killed instantly by the smoke, others trampled in the rush. Silence.

'Thank you,' said the man amid the carnage, ' I feel better for that.' As he left he handed me a hefty tip. I burned it.

Call me Kissinger

Like all careers in international peacemaking, mine began humbly with a trip to the supermarket. With the adroitness for which I am known, I passed through the sliding plate-glass door at the second attempt, and as I stood rubbing my elbow I beheld a man with the gold teeth and the leather jacket that denote in these parts a Russian trawlerman. He was trying to make himself understood to a checkout girl who cowered behind her scanner. He spoke no English, she no Russian, and tempers were fraying like the cuffs on my modish corduroys.

Just as in 1 BC the people of Judea had no notion who was lurking offstage in the wings of history, so Mr Russian Trawler and Miss Packyourbags were unaware that destiny had sent them a linguistic messiah.

You see, I studied Russian at school. And how my classmates scoffed at the time. 'Scoff,' they said as one. 'Ha ha,' they said. 'Do you imagine,' they said, 'that Russian will be of any use to man, beast or you in the long years ahead? Do you imagine that there is any demand this side of Vladivostok for fluency in an archaic, inflected, Cyrillic language?'

'*Da*,' I said. That floored them. Up they picked themselves and off they slunk to their grim little utilitarian economics classes, while I flung my babushka imperiously over my shoulder and returned to my study of the language of Pushkin and Samovar.

That was twenty-five years ago. A quarter of a century I have waited to justify learning the thirty-three letters of the Russian alphabet, and taming my tongue to words like *Zdravstvooeetye* which means hello and explains why Yeltsin hugs people rather than greeting them.

Meanwhile, back at the checkout things had grown critical. Russian eyeballs were bulging. Light glinted from gold teeth. Miss Checkout had mustered a glow to the cheeks which could have grilled a chop. Hearing about me the soft flutter of the wings of fate, I drew myself up to my full five foot four and prepared to intercede. In my mind I saw my schoolmates of yesteryear eating their words with a side-salad of envy.

Russian sentences bubbled up from the swamps of memory, many of them straight from my school textbook: 'I have a yellow bicycle'; 'The fat man is wearing a striped tie'; 'My brother is fond of ballet'; and, though I would not swear to the source of this one: 'Why are you coming so quickly, Pyetya?' I recalled all the words to 'Kalinka', and the night I sang it at the Dunsandel War Memorial Hall and danced like a cossack. I can still smell the geraniums that the organizer of the function brought to my hospital bed.

Anyway, now was my chance to put my knowledge to use. I eyeballed Mr Russian Trawlerman. '*Zdravstvooeetye*,' I said. Somewhere amid the frozen foods a pin dropped. Mr Trawlerman looked at me. Miss Checkout looked at me. He, she, I and time stood still.

'*Zdravstvooeetye*,' I said again and smiled in the manner of all international conciliators. It worked. Mr Trawlerman relaxed and unleashed a torrent of Russian. He clearly held some strong opinions which he reinforced with vigorous hand movements, several of which did not make contact with my flesh. He finished and leaned over me in a manner which made me unable to ignore what he had drunk for lunch.

'*Da*,' I said. Then, in case this seemed a little obsequious, I added, '*Nyet*'. That was all it took. In that traditional Russian gesture of friendship and respect he spat twice on the floor and left the supermarket.

While all about me gawped, I nonchalantly wrestled a trolley from the trolley-snake and went about my shopping as if nothing untoward had happened.

The other side of the fence

In a novel by David Lodge – but I can't remember which one and I'm damned if I'm going to look it up to get the details right. Getting details right is petty, retentive and prim, and, besides, details rarely tally with the purer truth of memory – a gaggle of professors of English goes down and dirty. Driven by gin and guilt they confess the titles of the great works of literature they have not read. *War and Peace*, says one and his colleagues gasp.

As the temperature goes up and the gin down, each strives to expose more thrilling ignorance than the other. The eventual winner is the prof of Renaissance drama who has never read *Hamlet*. (Don't bother to write and tell me I've got that wrong. That's how I remember it and it'll do me just fine. Even if it isn't what Lodge wrote it's what he would have written if he'd thought of it.)

So, anyway, the profs shake off the layers of lies of a life lived badly, and thus do what we all long to do in the small hours of the night where the truth squats beside us on the pillow and nags us to come clean: to return to the state of innocence where what we say is what we mean, where we laugh when we are happy and cry when we are sad, where Mummy knows best, rusks drop from heaven and where life is a naked romp in the sun and tomorrow doesn't exist.

Oh to fling off all the fibs and neuroses, the things we said to look good, the flatteries we let pass, each of them harmless in itself but building over the years into a shell that hardens into all we've got. (Yes, that's a quotation too, from by far the best of modern poets and if you haven't read him, tough, you should. He pins us down like grubs in a display case.)

All this then to introduce the woman who confessed to me today that she had never seen a *Star Wars* film. She felt, she said, guilty. That's what she said, 'Guilty'.

Rejoice woman, rejoice. Your guilt is but fear of solitude. You are suffering from the grief of the fat child who is last to be picked for a team. The grief of the loner, the outcast, the sheep trapped on the wrong side of the fence, desperate to rejoin the smug dumb herd. All around you stands the open world of possibility but you're desperate for captivity.

The wrong side of the fence is the place to be, always, and anyway, woman, you are not alone. I have never seen a *Star Wars* film either and nor do I intend to. And I shall tell you why. I have not seen a *Star Wars* film because I hate them. They're trashy seventies junk with special effects and I hate special effects more than I hate netball or Thai food or media liaison personnel. Anyone with a computer and bottle-bottom glasses can make special effects. They're like those ghastly kids at school who got extra marks for colouring in the title pages of their projects. Never mind that their projects had nothing to say. Never mind that they had culled the stuff straight from encyclopaedias. Their projects looked nice, so they won. It's the same with *Star Wars*.

Did you not see the footage of the 'people' rampaging through store-doors at opening time last week to do battle over what the world calls merchandise? Grown 'people' frantic for plastic swords that glow when you wallop them, and models of Darth Skywalker (*stet*, damn you, *stet*) with arms that actually move when you move them. Did you not see these images?

Boycott *Star Wars*. Go for truth, substance, beauty, independence, art that examines a life, that comes with no plastic merchandise, no sub-neanderthal hype. Go read *War and Peace*, for God's sake. Then write and tell me what it's about.

All day long I'd deedle-deedle-dum

Once upon a time I liked this woman a lot. Then I stopped liking her. As soon as I stopped liking her she started liking me. Now she has sent me a chain-letter. I don't understand.

This chain-letter goes by the name of a Nepali Tantra Totem. It contains the famous Nepali Instructions for Life, which are the drops of pure wisdom distilled from centuries of thinking by monks in monasteries on mountains. There's some inspiring stuff. For instance, No. 26 of the Instructions for Life: 'Read more books and watch less TV.' Or 28: 'Trust in God but lock your car.' Aeons of wisdom there. No. 15 of the forty-five indispensable Nepali Tantra Totem Instructions for Life is 'Call your mom.'

If I send this wisdom to 0–4 people my life will 'improve slightly', and presumably the lives of at least four Nepali moms will be enriched. If I send it to 5–9 people my life will 'improve to my liking', as opposed to improving not to my liking. 9–14 people and I will have at least five surprises in the

180

next three weeks. 15 or more people and 'life will improve drastically and everything I ever dreamed of will begin to take shape and I will become rich'. Thank you, monks.

If I were a rich man
All day long I'd deedle-deedle-dum . . .

That song is wrong. You don't have to be a rich man to deedle-deedle-dum. I deedle-deedle-dum all the time. For me deedle-deedle-dumming means staring at blank paper, walking the dogs and gawping.

Everyone wants to get rich. For most people that means winning the Lottery. Every day throughout the country a million sentences begin with, 'If I win the Lottery.' We imagine that winning the Lottery takes the strife out of life and replaces it with deedle-deedle-dumming. So it does. That's the trouble with it.

Anyone who wins the Lottery immediately buys a ranch house of hideous design and *en suite* everything in Surfers Paradise – and no place with a name like that could be anything but awful – slumps into a Lazyboy and gives himself to pleasure. What he meets is truth. He sees stretching before him a succession of days of endless sunshine, empty beaches, Australian cultural experiences and hours of deedle-deedle-dumming. And deedle-deedle-dumming – otherwise known as wool-gathering, doing nothing, lazing, sprawling, enjoying yourself, thinking, giving up thinking for drinking, musing, giving up musing for boozing, longing for dusk, dreading dawn, having the whole commercial chocolate box at one's mercy and realizing the thudding truth that chocolates are nice in anticipation but nasty as diet – is hell. In a matter of months the Lottery winner is pushing a bicycle round the central city, carrying bags of litter and talking to seagulls.

You need to be able to have everything that you want to realize that you don't want it, that the carrot which dangled in front of you and dragged you forward was a bad carrot, a carrotty mirage. The Lottery-winner ends up grasping the truth of dear old seedy Thoreau, the hermit-philosopher of the American backwoods who pronounced – God bless his dungarees and his little house on the prairie – that happiness increases in direct proportion to the things you can do without.

And the morals that emerge are all the old morals, the time-worn, shop-soiled tedious truths of travel being better than arrival, of hope springing eternal in the garden of human delusion. Lottery equals chain-letters, which equal, for that matter, communism, fascism, advertising or God.

I was supposed to forward the chain-letter within four days. If I failed to do so, unspeakable things would happen to me. That was five days ago. Ha. But I still don't understand why the woman sent it to me.

The barber's pole is fallen

The barber's shop delights me with its ancient leather chair, a sturdy thing that could have come from clubs where wealthy men talk wealthy things with other wealthy men and where no women go. And round a proper barber's chair a proper barber flits, a man of middle age and great discretion, snipping hair from fifty heads a day.

Repository of gossip, Mr Snips can turn his words to any subject any man can want. He soothes the souls of men and grooms their skulls and sells them cigarettes, and 'Was there something else, today, sir?' A barber's shop's a womb of men, a sure and certain refuge in a helter-skelter world where nothing is as once it was.

Although the vanity of men can crow as loud and high as cockerels, we middle-aged take little pride in hair. Our strands are few and thin and all we want is lightly up and down and over with the buzzing thing which looks to have been built for tiny sheep. Like gentle dentistry it is, a cossetting, a reassurance in a spiky world. It takes a mere ten minutes, then the softest brush across the neck, a little squirt of something fresh as flattery, the deft removal of the loose protective cape, the thin cascade of clippings to the floor, the brief exchange of cash, the 'Thank you, sir,' the opened door, the *au revoir*, and then the windy street once more with tiny hairs beneath the collar itching at the spine.

But O *tempora*! O *mores*! I must sing a song of doom. For the barber's shops are withering, the ancient chair is cracked, and with it go the cigarettes, the Brylcreem, combs and comfort of the past.

In suburbs where the houses cost a lot, the barber's stripey poles been taken down, and in his place has come a hairdresser, or worst of all a stylist. Where once the barber simply cut and talked he now does layering and tints, and other things I neither need nor understand. No longer is he Ken or Ron. His name is Gustave. No longer does he wear the sort of jacket favoured by the sellers of ice-cream, but rather now he greets me in a shirt without a collar. Designer stubble laid across his cheeks, he runs a little empire full of basins and shampoos with foreign names. The chairs that fill this horror shop resemble office furniture, and furthermore he hires a mass of Traceys and Charlenes to cut my hair. They fuss at me and preen and pat and as the noble Digby Anderson observed, the Traceys do not talk to me of politics or sport, but make enquiries how I'd like my hair. I say I'd like it cut. They think I've made a joke. Then little Gustave trots across and drenches me in cappuccino-breath, and wonders if perhaps a hint of bouffing here or gelling there might spruce me up and . . .

'Listen here, my friend. Atop this head of mine there isn't hair enough to stuff a mouse's duvet, and all I ask is that young Tracey gets the clippers out and treats me like a tiny patch of lawn. Just up and over, down and round the sides, a little bit of shaving at the neck, and I'll be off. And while she does the job she's free to talk of rugby or of politics, of boyfriends or of God, but never once is she to mention hair.'

That's what I want to say. Of course I do not say it. As Gustave plans the battle with my scalp I sit in smarting silence. Then Tracey tries to style and shape the hair I haven't got and then I rise and pay exactly twice what I once paid to Ron and Ken. I say goodbye to Gustave and I wander from the premises and then I turn and tap upon the window. And when the precious Gustave turns to look I place my fingers in among my hair and muss it up.

A pyrrhic victory, of course, a tiny self-defeating gesture of defiance to a world that's gone to pot, but worth it just to hear a stylist squeal.

Sing, baby, sing

Whenever I take a shower I think of Simon Monk. In 1969 in the hall at Brighton Grammar School, Simon Monk tested my voice.

He pressed a key on the piano. 'Sing that,' said Monk. I sang that.

'No,' said Monk. He pressed another key. 'You're singing this.' The note sounded familiar.

'Sing this,' said Monk. I sang this.

'Next,' said Monk and I slunk off into a splendid thirty-year sulk. For Simon Monk was wrong and every morning underneath the amniotic pleasure of the shower I prove him wrong. Coccooned in steam I pavarotti song on song which shake the taps and set the window rattling. The cat, whose delight in watching me shower makes it unique within the scheme of things, reverberates with relish. My repertoire is broad but every shower includes 'Mine eyes have seen the glory of the corpse of Simon Monk.'

But thanks to Monk I'm shy of public singing. The national anthem has me mumbling at my shoes. It's all the dirge deserves, of course, but this is no world to hide virtues in.

But then came Mr Asia. He moved into the port in which I live and just to taunt me he opened up a bar, a little bar with cheap formica tables, beer in cans, a woman out the back who fries the prawns and, hanging from the roof, a karaoke screen. His clientele is mainly men from foreign lands who fish for squid.

I steered well clear of Mr Asia's karaoke joint until last Saturday, when Jon and I foregathered at the great Volcano, a restaurant awash with stars from Access Radio, and where the corks go pop till late into the night. We ate two plates of kidneys soaked in sherry and then set out to patronise a bar or two, and somehow as we walloped down the street we found our way to the forfended place where Mr Asia welcomed us with arms as broad as Christmas. A group of Portuguese made room for us, a small Korean sailor gave us prawns, we bought our cans of beer, then someone shoved a mike into my hand and asked if I would sing.

O Simon Monk, I thought, where are you now? You've held my life in thrall for thirty years, you've squatted on my neck and crushed my soul and how I hope you do a dreary job. I hope you check accounts for companies that manufacture surgical appliances. I hope you wear a dark-brown suit and live in some depressing suburb always under cloud. I hope you own a shelf of Swedish books.

For now my time had come. 'Oi, Mr Asia, play "The Green Green Grass Of Home".'

The oriental version of the song went far too fast. My old house was still standing while the screen was stepping down from the train. I shut my eyes and carried on. And then, somehow, and somewhere deep in my neurosis, a blockage burst and through the breach came flooding notes as rich as velvet. I was transported. Passion poured from me, a great forbidden river of emotion. As I drew out the final notes I raised my hand to fend off the knickers that the woman who fried the prawns was sure to throw at me. I opened my eyes.

Jon was laughing, the Koreans were bent over their prawns, the Portuguese had gone, and on the screen the video was halfway through 'Delilah'. Mr Asia was applauding, but then he owns the bar.

I handed him the mike and toddled home to bed, the shade of Simon Monk a yard behind me, his footsteps keeping time with mine and muttering the words of Samuel Taylor Coleridge:

Swans sing before they die. 'Twere no bad thing
Did certain persons die before they sing.

Back to the beach

A few million years ago, our forebears hauled themselves out of the sea and lay panting on the beach. And every year, at around this time, we go back there to do the same thing. It is a pilgrimage.

The beach is elemental. Earth meets water, water meets sky, and in the sky stands fire.

Few things live on the beach. The sand is strewn with the translucent bodies of little jellyfish which pop when you tread on them. Gulls prey on the shells and crabs that didn't make it back. Between the fertility of the sea and the fertility of the land, the beach is a barren strand.

And yet, despite the sunburn and the insects and the sand in the sandwiches, year after year we return to the beach, and we lie on the sand and we turn to the heat and the light like reptiles. Toes and bodies snuggle into the sand's warmth, for the beach is a sensual place. It is a place of flesh.

Little children sport in the shallows, naked as birth and squealing. They build things of sand, they fight and they bury their fathers. They will spend the rest of their lives doing much the same things.

It is the teenagers who are most in harmony with

the beach. They parade lean, taut bodies and shriek together in the surf and play sex games in thigh-deep water. Or else they wear wetsuits like a second skin and seek to govern the waves. Seen from the beach they look like seals.

Their parents look like walruses. Time has stolen their lean and taut and replaced it with something that sags. No longer can they play volleyball or sex in the shallows, so they wade out deeper, rising on tiptoe with each swell of water to delay the moment that shivers the crotch.

Then they plunge, swim a few strokes and become instantly bored, for the sea is no good for swimming. There is nothing to hold on to, and nowhere to head for but the horizon. Faced with the aimlessness of ocean, they return through youth and frisbees to the beach and collapse on a towel to ogle or eat sandwiches.

Those who are still older do not undress at all. They bask in air and sun like plants, or they totter to the water's edge to paddle with the very little ones in their own second babyhood.

Over the course of any year we accrete things which we consider important. We gain money, status and vanities. At the beach we take them off again. We may spend the year caring about sport, but the games that we play at the beach don't matter. The beach is good for us.

In this elemental, physical world, the high court judge becomes an old man with bumpy legs. The youth whom he lectured becomes king.

The beach is the edge of the world. On the

horizon a huge and tiny freighter is held immobile by the afternoon. A black dog bounds and barks through the wavelets. It is simple and happy. A gull arcs perfect on the air. Its mewing means nothing. Like the sun and the sea and the land and the air and the people and the dog, the gull is.

Dig it and dung it

Our society is sick. And, as many a social commentator has commentated, the reason that we are poor in both pocket and soul is that no one these days grows vegetables.

Back when a pound was neither a kilo nor a dollar but something so dependable that you could marry it, every dad had a yard at the back called the backyard where he grew peas, potatoes, parsnips, pavlovas, everything in short that modern man buys from the supermarket.

In those days of huge families Dad would come home from work in his braces and collarless shirt, and without even pausing to put trousers on he would be out the back pulling his carrots.

But not any more. As a child of the late twentieth century I suspect that I am typical. Not only do I not grow vegetables, I don't eat them unless they are disguised by salt, grease or, ideally, meat. By vegetables I mean, of course, chips.

On those more or less annual occasions when I crave green stuff I open a packet of frozen peas, take a good deep health-giving sniff and throw them away.

But, last week at that cultural melting-pot the Volcano Café, I met a man who grows vegetables. He evangelized for vegetables. He carried soil samples around with him. He even had cauliflower ears. I made a little joke about those ears but he didn't laugh. He wasn't the laughing type. He was a priest, a pastor of parsnips, a reverend of roots.

Passing around soil samples from under his fingernails he preached the joys of horticulture. A crowd gathered. I listened and I was converted.

The moment I reached home I dived under the house to ferret out my gardening tools. In no time at all I had assembled a spade and a stick. The stick may once have been a hoe.

As every countryman knows the best soil lies under the tallest thistles. I selected a stand of thistles like a Scottish rainforest and set about them with a will and the stick. The stick broke. The thistles didn't. I slung my stick, seized my spade, turned my sod and dug the thistles in.

The dogs watched in mute fascination. Half an hour, a heavy sweat, and I had no more thistles. Instead there stretched away into the distance a thrilling expanse of brown, tilled earth, as sweet as God made it, and almost a metre square. My vegetable patch. My direct line to nature.

Friable is the word. The best soil, friable soil, crumbles between the fingers like crumble. My soil was so friable you could have biffed it in with the bacon. It held worms so big the dogs barked at them. I sifted the good earth through my fingers and had visions of terrific carrots, triffid beans and marrows like nuclear submarines.

In the supermarket I wanted to buy every seed in the rack but at $2 a packet, two packets equalled my annual fresh vegetable budget. Nevertheless with over 800 lettuce seeds to the packet I realized I could recoup my money with a roadside stall – indeed at a dollar a piece I could turn a $798 profit – so I splashed out on the seeds of lettuce, carrots, beans and frozen peas.

In fifty-five days, according to the packet, I would have plump lettuce. That meant 2 December. By 15 December my cup would run over with stringless beans. Carrots and peas would follow before Christmas. I felt myself blossom in pocket and soul.

Back at my market garden in a warm, vegetable-encouraging nor'westerly gale, I dug a little lettuce trench in the friable and tore open the foil packet with my teeth. Lettuce seeds are remarkably small and light. Several of them settled in the trench where I patted them happily down.

Back indoors I turned my diary to 2 December and scribbled a note to myself to hunt down approximately 780 fat lettuces up against the fence to the south-east.

The carrot seeds were tiny too so I just planted the pea seeds and the bean seeds. To the untrained eye these seeds are strikingly similar in size and weight to actual beans and peas. They must be among evolution's errors. It would take a hurricane to broadcast them.

The carrots hit the soil the next day. I couldn't

recall exactly where I had planted my other seeds, and, besides, the dogs had done a little digging of their own, so I just dropped the carrots in here and there and smoothed the plot.

That was three days ago. According to the packets none of the seeds should germinate within a week, but my friable is so rich that already I've got green things sprouting all over. I shall water them, nurture them, watch over them with a mother's care and then eat them. It's a wonderful world.

Underground heroes

When I opened the paper this morning the years fell away.

Suddenly I was thirteen years old once more, a boy in shorts, bright of eye, weak of chin and with my torso already hinting at the musculature that was to earn me the nickname Podge.

It's all to do with the *Guinness Book of Records*. That book was the bible of my childhood. Every night, in the swelter of my suburban bed, as the mosquitoes hummed and I hummed along with them, I turned the oracular pages of the *Guinness Book of Records* and I took its wisdom to my bosom.

Thanks to those long tropical nights, I can, to this day, recount a litany of records at the drop of a hat. Indeed, at the tail end of a dinner party only the other evening, a popsy dropped her hat and before you could say narcolept I had pinned her to the wall and was informing her, among other things, that the most poisonous creature on this planet is not a snake, nor yet a scorpion, nor even a talkback host, but a frog. To be precise it is the Colombian Tree Arrow Frog.

I let her know – and I could tell she was

fascinated from the way she kept looking over my shoulder – that 0.000000003 milligrams of the venom from a Colombian Tree Arrow Frog will kill a horse. Her eyes bulged like those of the frog itself as I elaborated on the horrors of Colombian pony-trekking.

In my youth the *Guinness Book of Records* so obsessed me that I asked nothing more of life than to be in it. Then one night I read in its pages of a man in Minnesota who had thrown a fresh egg, and of another man, also in Minnesota, who had caught that egg. The distance between the two Minnesotans was 156 feet. No egg-thrower and catcher in history had stood further apart.

A scent wafted by me. I flared a nostril and caught the heady whiff of glory.

In those days there came no lapse between thought and action and in no time at all I found myself in the back garden with an egg. By the light of a winter moon I could make out the residence of Mr and Mrs Braddock, an imposing brick bungalow perhaps 200 feet away.

The egg proved a splendid missile. Back in bed I basked in the knowledge that I had a record within my throwing range, and I slid into the bliss of sleep to the lullaby of Mrs Braddock's alarmed soprano and Mr Braddock's bass threats delivered in pyjamas to a wide and empty sky.

The following day I skipped the many miles to school with a song in my heart and a dozen eggs in my bag. I knew that I had only to recruit an egg-catcher and fame was assured.

Colin Potts was not, perhaps, the most co-ordinated child at Brighton Grammar School, but he was the most easily bullied. So it was Colin Potts who spent his lunchtime on the school football pitch stationed some 200 feet away from me, and it was I who wore my arm to a frazzle biffing egg after egg for Colin Potts to catch, and it was Mrs Potts who sent my mother a dry-cleaning bill that made her gasp.

All this, then, to explain the pang of memory that stabbed me this morning when I opened the paper. On the international pages stood the headline 'Briton lays down record'.

Mr Geoff Smith, aged thirty-seven, has found his way into the good book by spending four and a half months in a beer garden. Such a feat used to be called studying at university, but, unlike a student, Mr Smith spent those months 2.7 metres underground in a wooden coffin. Only a tube connected him with the outside world, a tube down which his friends and family poured food and encouragement and, on the 142nd day, a torrent of congratulation. For on that day he shattered the world live-burial record previously held by an American. Forty-one days before that, Mr Smith had broken the European record held by a Mrs Emma Smith, also of Great Britain. The coincidence of surnames between the former European-record holder and the present world-record holder is explained by the fact that Emma is Geoff's mother.

I don't know about yours but my heart swells. While you and I have maundered through our days, the Smiths have made something of their lives. They have seized fate by the throat and have wrung from it a place in the halls of fame. Something thunderously human inhabits the Smith spine, something great and good, and like me you will rejoice to know that Geoff has sired three little Smiths. Let us hope that the DNA remains vigorous and that one day we will read of the horizontal subterranean exploits of at least one of these three.

What suffuses the Smith soul is the same sterling stuff which drives one man around the world in a balloon, and another to the South Pole with only a cellphone for company. When I read of such derring-do, the years fall away like leaves and I stand once more in short trousers with an egg in my hand, a football pitch stretching away before me, a spattered Colin Potts a distant speck and glory hovering on the edges of my vision.

Go home

It is two in the morning. Lights illumine empty streets, the nightshift on the wharf loads a ship with a giant crane and popular music pumps through the walls of my house. I can feel it in my feet and spine. Someone in the street is having a party.

I love parties but I do not love this party. I would like to sleep. I tried holding the pillow over my head. I burrowed beneath the duvet. I counted sheep, turned on to my right side and my left side and my chest, but the sheep carried guitars and the bed thrummed with the beat and I grew angry. I rose and padded naked to the deck. The warm night air pleased my skin but carried with it the news that we all live in a yellow submarine.

I do not want to go round and complain because I too have held parties. When the bank generously bought me my first house I invited people to help me warm it. I also warned the neighbours. One splendid elderly man was all tolerance. 'Go ahead, Joe, have your party,' he said, 'Get the young people round and have a good time. I'll just call the police.' He didn't, of course. He and his wife were among the first to arrive. They brought wine and a plate of scones and they stayed until midnight.

But now it is well past midnight and the dogs are nervous. They do not know why I have got out of bed and the noise unsettles them. They sniff the air and are ready to defend the house, but the enemy has no form. The larger dog whines in confusion.

Come on, feel the noise
Girls rock the boys

I can feel the noise. It brings to mind a fancy-dress party I went to last year in one of the nicer suburbs. I do not recall what I wore, but Dave the host dressed as the young Queen Victoria. It was an exact likeness, except that Victoria was a small woman. Dave is a lock.

At an early hour of the morning the noise-control officer visited. He was not a lock. He wore a sad uniform and a moustache that did not command respect. He never stood a chance.

Dave came swanning to the door, his tiara glistening, his make-up impeccable, his orange organza ball gown billowing behind him. He dwarfed Mr Noise-control who gripped his torch tightly.

'Are you the host?'

'Darling,' exclaimed Dave, and he clutched the little man to him, lifted him squirming from the floor and planted a kiss on his cheek that sounded like one of those rubber things you use to unblock drains. The noise-control man went away and we were all happy.

But the noise-man was there because sober souls were sitting unhappy in their houses round about and cursing the noise, just as I am doing now. I suppose the definition of a good party is one to which you are invited. All others stink.

'Can you hear the drums, Fernando?'

I can hear the drums. I could jab wads of wet toilet paper in my ears but then I would not hear the alarm in the morning and I have to be up by seven.

It must be a middle-aged party, for the songs are from the sixties and seventies. I recognize them all. For each of us, I suspect, popular music will always mean the stuff which played when our hormones ached. In the turbulence of youth we absorb words and tunes that time cannot erase.

In a play by, I think, Noël Coward, a character spoke of the potency of cheap music. He was right, because cheap music is primitive. It embodies the most urgent urges of our lives in rhythms which echo the beat of the blood.

Like certain smells, songs unleash floods of memory. Right now the Police are singing, 'Don't stand so, don't stand so, don't stand so close to me' and the song hurls me back twenty years to a dank garden in Fontainebleau where I was crouching drunk on a stone pillar among bushes. I was pretending to be a griffon. It had something to do with love. I can smell the smoke in the air of that night, feel the waxy texture of the leaves that brushed against me, sense the breathless all-importance of desire. The Police are now middle-aged and so am I.

It is three o'clock and I can hear guests leaving. They are loud and happy. With sentiment dripping from every word, the Seekers are singing 'The Carnival Is Over', and I hope they are right.

Creep into thy narrow bed

Do you fret about apostrophes? When the menu says 'curry with vegetable's' do you froth?

Well, it is time to give up. Stop frothing. We've lost. The illiterates have won and it just doesn't matter. They have swarmed down from the hills with horns on their helmets and oaths on their breath, and they have ransacked the citadel, burned the library, ravaged the virgins, broken the necks of the vintage bottles and killed the little apostrophe. And they don't care. They care for their cellphones and their foreign bottled lager but they do not care for the apostrophe, and because they are so many and so heathen you might as well stop resisting.

Let the long contention cease.
Geese are swans, and swans are geese.
Let them have it how they will.
Thou art tired; best be still.

By their signs shall ye know them and their signs are everywhere: Egg's for sale; Hot Chip's; Womens Toilets'.

Using the apostrophe to indicate ownership is a

modern convention. To be sure, Shakespeare used the apostrophe, but only to indicate a missing letter, just as it is used in other languages. When Shakespeare wrote St James's Street he inserted an apostrophe only because he had omitted an *e*. The possessive use of the apostrophe was unheard of before 1725 and much derided thereafter. But you and I know in our bones that when the possessive apostrophe dies, then civilization will wither, and we will be left atop a heap of rubble and we will be left lamenting.

How fiercely we once fought for it. I smile when I recall how we mocked the shops that sold sausage's, and how we wrote ferocious letters to newspapers, and how we who laboured in the classroom expended gallons of red ink circling childrens and childrens' in children's essays and did not count the cost. But it has got us nowhere. And now it is time to give up. We have lost.

Creep into thy narrow bed,
Creep, and let no more be said.

The illiterates will tell you that we don't need the possessive apostrophe. They will say, if they can be bothered to say anything, that putting an apostrophe after an *s* to indicate a possessive plural makes no sense because no letter is omitted. They speak true. And they will say that we do not need the apostrophe to make our meaning clear because we get by perfectly well with the spoken language, despite the apostrophe being inaudible. And again they speak true, but there are greater causes than truth and the apostrophe is one of those.

Nevertheless the war is over and it is lost. Illiteracy has won the day. All you can do is to hold up your head in the knowledge that you fought the good fight and that your wounds are in the front.

They out-talked thee, hissed thee, tore thee.
Better men fared thus before thee.

But, in the end, what greater thing can a man do than stand and fight for punctuation? Though the apostrophe may be irrational, irrelevant, confusing, pointless, modern and wrong, a man can love it more dearly than he loves life itself. Do you, as you read these words, feel something that swells in the chest and stirs in the loins like a lizard quickened by the sun, something that goes beyond reason, something that says with quiet strength, 'I am and I believe'? You do?

Charge once more, then, and be dumb.
Let the victors, when they come,
When the forts of folly fall,
Find thy body by the wall.

Beat the beet

I'm going to have a silver beet party. You are invited. It's BYO.

A few months ago I wrote of the intensive preparations that went into my vegetable patch. Clearly my return to the soil struck a chord, and many readers have since asked me how the harvest has gone. This column is dedicated to both of those readers.

Firstly, I believe in forgiveness. So, I hereby and publicly forgive the prankster who scattered the weed seeds. It was a good joke and in case he or she hasn't dared to return to check on his handiwork I can tell him or her that it succeeded. Rarely can so dense a crop of weeds have been raised in so small a space.

Baby weeds and baby vegetables are remarkably similar in colour, and I murdered many an infant lettuce until a horticultural neighbour taught me what was what. Thereafter keeping the weeds down became a simple matter of eight hours' hoeing a day.

The hoe is an entertaining little tool. Mine can skirt around a thistle for several hours, but give it the sniff of a bean plant and it will scythe the life out of it before you can say unprintable. I found, in the end, that the best way to weed was by hand, starting at the end of a row and working backwards along it, pulling out the weeds as I went and taking care to tread heavily on the vegetable plants behind me.

My first crop was peas. Pea plants have endearing little tendrils that grope blindly in the air, like the hands of orphan babies. I suspended a string above the row of peas and to that string I tied other strings, strings that swung in the breeze for the peas to seize. And the orphan peas that seized in the breeze so pleased me that I wrote a little poem about them which I shall spare you.

Three months after sowing I had a mass of fat pea-pods which supplied me and the horticultural neighbour with evening meals for the whole of one Tuesday. All the same, I can tell you now that nothing compares with the succulence of a pea picked fresh from the garden, apart, of course, from the succulence of a frozen pea.

My dwarf stringless beans lived up to their name. They showed no hint of string and with the aid of a magnifying glass I gathered many a bulging thimbleful.

Lettuces flopped. I grew a popular variety with a crisp balled heart and flavoursome buttery leaves which goes by the name of Slug's Delight. With gratifying speed the lettuce pushed their buttery heads up through the soil, but each evening, as darkness fell over Lyttelton, one could catch on the

208

wind the dulcet notes of a slughorn, followed by the steady trudge of the slug battalions. Down from the hills the slugs came rumbling, frolicking and tumbling, and they settled on my crisp balled hearts and my flavoursome buttery leaves.

The crunch of slug-jaws was such that sleep was impossible. In the end I rigged up a little mai-mai where I would sit up all night with the dogs, brewing cup after cup of whisky on a little spirit stove and occasionally raising to my shoulder the ancient slug-gun and firing blindly into the vegetable patch. The dogs would bound out to gather the corpses and lay them reverently at my feet, but the cause was hopeless. If you've seen the film *Zulu* you'll know exactly what I mean. In the end I ate only one lettuce and it looked like a string vest. Deep in its raddled heart I found a slug, gently snoring and sporting a look of beatific satisfaction. I tossed it on the barbecue, heard it squeal, watched it shrivel, laughed a hollow laugh and fed it to the dogs.

But all was not disaster. Graeme told me to grow silver beet. You can't go wrong with silver beet, said Graeme. Even a moron could grow silver beet, said Graeme. I wasn't sure I liked the tone of that last line, but in deference to Graeme I planted six silver beet seeds. And from those seeds came six strong plants which grew like a rainforest, their crinkled leaves swelling visibly, powering un-stoppably skywards. My silver beet swelled into slug-shrugging monsters which dwarfed the dwarf beans, terrorized the orphan peas and shaded the deck. Of late the silver beet has taken to knocking at night on the window of the bedroom where the dogs and I cower together behind the chest of drawers.

Yes, the silver beet was a triumph, but I hate the stuff. It tastes of school cabbage. If you'd like some, please come to the party. BYO axe.

So, *where are they?*

I was reared on a television programme called *Tomorrow's World*. Raymond Baxter the presenter looked like an accountant but lacked the fizzing personality. On *Tomorrow's World* he prodded gizmos with his ballpoint pen and explained how they would revolutionize my life. I remember house-cleaning robots, self-steering cars and backpacks for personal flight. I wanted them all right then. But Raymond Baxter patted me on the head and told me I must wait.

The date I would have to wait for was always in the middle of the 1990s. The nineties defined the future. They were unthinkably distant. The nineties would bring ease. In the nineties all drudgery would be done by machine. The only industry would be leisure. The world would hum with technology. My job would be to wear a sort of thin purple wetsuit and loll in a hammock. Once in a while I would loll across to the orgasmatron.

In the brave new world of the nineties, the word labour would be obsolete. The dictionary would define it as:

    i. an activity indulged in by ancient civilizations

ii. pain suffered by women in a primitive system of reproduction

iii. the name of an extinct political party.

The nub of it all was the labour-saving device. Work was bad and leisure was pleasure. Never mind that people like work. Never mind that people dread unemployment. Never mind that people cling to jobs like liferafts in the great ocean of pointlessness. Never mind that people love to grumble and work gives them something to grumble about. Never mind the wisdom of great thinkers like the bloke whose name I can't remember and can't find in the dictionary of quotations who said, 'He who chops his own firewood warms himself twice.' No, never mind truth, we must make people idle. By the time the nineties came round, indolence would be in.

Well it isn't in. As far as I can tell, people seem to loll less than they used to and work more, probably because they like it. Nor do I see around me the gizmos that Raymond prodded with his pen and promised me I would have. Nearly all the labour-saving devices that exist today, existed when Raymond was a mere gleam in his mother's oestrogen. And those same labour-saving devices still don't save labour.

Take, for example, my vacuum cleaner. I wish you would. It has the same brand-name as a chainsaw but is much less fun. Nevertheless, when I bought it I thought it would be fun. I took it home, assembled its famously long wand – and why for God's sake is it called a wand? The only magic this machine managed was to make me part with $450 – plugged it in and got wanding. After two minutes, the dogs had gone crazy, my back ached and the carpet looked just as it always did. The only way I found to prove that the vacuum cleaner was working was to lay cat-biscuits on the floor and race the dogs to them. Or else I took the thingy off the wand-end and sucked lumps of my calf-muscle. It was vaguely exciting. I also enjoyed, for reasons which puzzle me but might intrigue Freud, the little pedal that retracted the cord like a rattle-snake.

Otherwise the thing was, is and always will be a waste of time. The only dirt it picks up is dust and dust is good for us. Get rid of dust and people start getting allergies to things like mites and oxygen. Dust is also useful. I can never find a pen near the phone so I write notes in it. As far as I am concerned, anything that isn't big enough to trip over isn't dirt. And if it is big enough to trip over you can't pick it up with a vacuum cleaner. Quentin Crisp, whom I also can't find in the dictionary of quotations, said, I think, more or less, that there was never any need to do housework. After the first few years the dust didn't get any worse.

The only function of my vacuum cleaner and many another labour-saving device is not to save labour but to create it. First, someone has to labour to make it. Then, the buyer has to labour in order to pay for it. Thirdly, once he has bought it, the buyer feels obliged to do labour that he didn't feel the need to do before. And so the economy swells and feasts upon itself and the balloon grows and we all work harder and the century accelerates towards its climax and tomorrow's extraordinary world is nothing like the one that Raymond Baxter promised.

Perhaps we should be grateful.

Weird stuff

A brace of young Mormons visited me the other day, dark-suited, soft-spoken and both called Elder. My dogs rose from the sofa to bark but the two young men did not falter. I invited them in and they took off their rucksacks and perched on the edge of the dog-warm sofa. Then they quietly and courteously tried to make a Mormon of me.

Elder and Elder's first question was whether I believed in a supreme being. I said I didn't. Nevertheless they spun me their missionary patter.

All religious belief is irrational. That doesn't make it wrong. Love is irrational too, and so is laughter. Life without love or laughter would be a pallid thing.

Any man's religion is his affair and his alone, but if he tries to foist that religion on to me then it becomes my affair. He has become a door-to-door salesman and I am entitled to study the goods. The goods that the Mormons have to sell are weird and shonky.

In the Mormon Visitor Centre in Salt Lake City, Utah, a glass box like a vast aquarium holds a life-size model of the church's founder, Joseph Smith.

A recording tells how in 1830 Smith was praying on a mountainside when lo, an angel of the Lord, one Moroni, appeared unto him. At this point a bright light illuminates the aquarium.

The recording explains how the angel gave Smith some golden plates with church rules written on them. Smith memorized what they said. This was fortunate, because by the time he returned from the mountain he didn't have the golden plates any more. Nevertheless, it is on those plates that Mormonism, a.k.a. the Church of Jesus Christ of Latterday Saints, is founded.

I asked the two Elders whether it was true that Joseph Smith had lost the golden plates.

'They were taken back,' said Elder.

I asked them if they accepted the theory of evolution. They said they did, but when I asked if we were descended from apes they said no. They believed, they said, in Adam and Eve.

'What, literally?' I asked.

They nodded. 'I guess we kind of believe in evolution and Adam and Eve,' explained Elder.

Mormonism embraces a welter of far greater absurdities than this, many of them sinister. Furthermore, it is a religion which preys on the vulnerable. Some Russian sailors are stranded in the port where I live. They have no money and are far from home. Elder and Elder told me with pride that this week they baptised one of these sailors.

Elder and Elder are gentle, credulous, serious, law-abiding people. They have given two years of their lives to rent a house in New Zealand and pad the streets in search of converts. People mock them, threaten them, abuse them. People like me challenge their ridiculous beliefs. Through all this, they speak quietly and if things get rough they move away and pray for their aggressors.

A society of people like Elder and Elder would be free of crime and violence. It would also be hateful.

The Elders and I parted amiably. In the windy sunshine I watched them climb the neighbour's steps. They had dog-hair all over the backs of their black suits.

A Parisian pig

I love the 'briefly' bits, the juicy single-paragraph items in the newspaper about something nasty that has happened to a foreigner who lives so far away that I don't have to expend any energy feeling guilt, sympathy or any of the other emotions that we're supposed to feel lots of but which aren't anywhere near as much fun as the real emotions such as anger, greed and delight at another's distress. No, the shorts are splendid because I'm free to chuckle at a Belgian decapitated by a frozen chicken, and frankly it's more good news like that that this country needs rather than the weeping and wailing and gnashing of ganglions over the fiscal deficit and unemployment and the decline of women's rugby league.

So when I read in the shorts this morning of a hunter in France who was killed by a stag which he was not unreasonably trying to murder, I thought ha ha and inhaled another spoonful of my Tasti Blueberry Crunch. But as I chewed, my mind slid back twenty years to a clearing in a forest outside Paris where stood a derelict caravan and a dirty little tent which belonged to Philippa but which I had borrowed to do a bit of solitary-adventurer stuff around Europe, the purpose of which was to get it over with as quickly as possible before heading home to tell people lies about it.

Well, courage has always been my long suit, particularly when alone in a tent in a foreign forest with night falling and the wind soughing in the trees and nameless things with grins and teeth flitting between branches, so I just curled in the sleeping bag, hugged my knees like lovers and went in for a bit of quietly courageous whimpering, alleviated by swigs from a plastic bottle of nerve tonic ordinaire.

Sleep seized me well before dawn. The next thing I heard was a snuffle-grunt. It was the sort of snuffle-grunt one doesn't ignore. Not for me the sleepy roll-over, the groan, the slow ascent from the deep waters of sleep to the bright cold air of consciousness. Rather, my flight-or-fight response, which has always favoured the first half of the formula, rendered me instantly awake, eyes pricked, ears gaping and my body rigid as a tentpole. I also cunningly stopped breathing.

Another snuffle-grunt, huge, breathy and dis-satisfied, sounded just beyond the opening of the tent. Then silence, bowel-churning silence. I slithered from the sleeping bag and inched open the zip on the tent. I expected to be rushed. Nothing. I eased my head out from the opening like one of the more cautious brands of tortoise and met, at a distance of approximately a metre, a wild boar. It had murderous intentions and tusks.

My options were several. I could shrink back into

my tent and wait to die, I could run away through the forest clad only in terror or I could do the sensible thing and attack the beast, wrestling it on to its back and then sticking it through the heart with a piece of plastic cutlery. I shrank back into the tent.

The boar had an amusing sense of drama. It snuffled around the perimeter of the tent grunting. I could only wait. I heard it pause to plan its attack. From my rucksack I drew a notebook, wrote the date, left everything to mother, signed my name and felt my bowels stir.

Thirty minutes later I opened the tent. In front of me, no boar. Round the sides of the tent, no boar. I stood naked in the dappled green of a forest dawn, raised my arms to the skies and whooped with the joy of being alive.

Across the clearing a man was sitting on the steps of the derelict caravan. He held a handful of bread from which the boar was calmly feeding.

Safety

I am suspected of wanting to kill children. My means of execution is a deck.

Some months ago when I was briefly flush with lolly I paid an architect to design me a deck, and a builder to build it. Both did a fine job, so fine a job indeed that I am now bedecked and broke. One part of the deck has fixed wooden seating round its rim to create a conversation pit and there, over the last few months, I have spent many a summer evening with friends, dogs and gin and we have tired the sun with talking and sent it down the sky. In short, the deck is a triumph.

If, however, I am ever to sell the house, I need to be able to prove that my triumphant deck is legal. So I rang the council and they sent a deckchecker to check the deck. He rattled its rivets, he wobbled its noggins and then he placed his chin between his thumb and his first two fingers in the manner of one engaged in thought, and he said no.

I said what, and he said no again and he pointed at the seating and said it had to go. Children, said he, could climb on to the seating, haul themselves on to the guardrail and dive to their deaths. I pointed out the cushion of unmown grass ten feet below, but Mr Deckcheck was unmoved. This was, said he, an unsafe deck.

I invited him to scour my house for children. He declined, on the grounds that, though I may be barren, my successors in this residence – deck-checkers talk like that – might be fecund. They might spawn hordes of little ones all of whom would like nothing better than to climb on to the seats and fling themselves into the grassy arms of eternity. The seating, said he, was unsafe seating and it had to go.

I argued of course. I argued that anyone who bought the house could see for themselves the lethal seating and choose not to buy. I further argued that my garden, like everyone else's garden, was full of trees which children with a deathwish could climb and tumble from at will. Deckchecker stood adamant, bolstered from behind by the immoveable weight of bureaucracy.

If, I asked, I were to remove the fixed seating and replace it with seating which was not fixed but which stood in the same place and which in-corporated little ladders to make it easier for kiddies to clamber on to, along with perhaps a stoup of holy water so they could make their final oblations before crossing the bourn from which no traveller returns, would that be all right? That, said Deckchecker, would be just dandy. Just so long as it wasn't fixed.

Therefore, I said, if I were to unfix the lethal seating, but leave it where it was, that would be all

222

right too. Yes, said Deckcheck, it would. So I did, and it was. The deck looks exactly the same as it did on the day that the deckchecker came and found it lethal, only now I have a pretty little certificate to certify that it is safe and legal.

And having given me my certificate, Deckcheck toddled off to wage his war on unsafeness. He set out on his mission to check every deck, fence every swimming pool, secure every seat-belt. If he has his way he will fell every tree, drain every stream, lock every medicine chest and ban sharp cutlery. And he will build for us a country of such anodyne safety, that not one of us will any longer need to be responsible for ourselves or for our children. Deck-check will care for us. He will eradicate chance, banish fate, and when finally we grow so bored that we fling ourselves from our collective decks into the everlasting night of nothing, he will mark the event with a nice, orderly little certificate.

223

Dancing with Destiny

C.B. Fry was the golden boy of the Edwardian era. By the age of forty-one, Fry had gained a first-class degree in classics, broken the world long-jump record, played cricket and soccer for England and been offered the throne of Albania. In addition he was considered the best ballroom dancer of his generation.

Now, when I point out that I too am forty-one I think you will agree that the parallels between my life and Fry's are too great to ignore. Admittedly Fry may have got a slight lead on me on the academic and sporting fronts, and he's also nudged ahead in throne-offers, but I believe that even old C.B. would acknowledge that on the dancefloor I take some beating.

Picture me then, if you would, at the society wedding of the year in Christchurch, leaning against a banister in my treble-breasted lambswool, the essence of suave. My eyes have that half-closed Lawrence-of-Arabia look which steals over me late at parties. In each hand I idly clutch a bottle of the host's champagne. Another protrudes from my pocket at a rakish angle. Around the ballroom

224

women visibly struggle to resist my allure. It says much for the women at this wedding that all have so far succeeded. But as the evening wears on I can sense the throbs of yearning in their breasts like the pulse of subterranean music.

Only one woman has dared to address me. 'You've got soup on your tie,' she said. Words can mask the strongest feelings. When you are in tune with the female psyche you see beyond words.

'I know,' I said, and winked at her. She understood, gave a little nervous snort that bystanders might have mistaken for derision, and melted back into the throng, her vital signs a-flutter.

I tongued my tie, openly, arrogantly. It tasted fine. I lingered over it, sucking the last of goodness from the viscose-and-rayon mix with its understated Mickey Mouse motif. I was conscious of eyes flicking my way. I waited. I did not have to wait long.

Barely three hours had flown by when out from the dancefloor came Destiny. Destiny wore a frock of shot silk. The bullet-holes gave glimpses of flesh that would have sent a weaker man to his knees. A woman of substance, glowing from the waltz. 'Destiny,' I whispered.

'You're drunk,' said Destiny.

I have seen it so often, the way women conceal their lust behind abuse. I merely smiled my knowing smile and swayed to an ancient internal rhythm. I would let Destiny take her course. She eased the bottles from my grasp. After a brief and sensuous struggle I let myself be guided by her will.

She unloaded my pockets of their burden, as symbolic an act as you could wish to see. When she pulled the bundle of the host's cigars from my inside pocket I could see she was impressed.

'Come on,' she said, 'let's dance,' and I allowed myself to be led to the floor, pausing only to trip deftly over a potted palm. Awe cleared instant space for us in the crowded marquee. The band was hard at it. I sensed the shade of C.B. Fry prodding me in the kidneys. 'Strut your stuff,' said old C.B.

Dancing, said George Bernard Shaw, is the perpendicular expression of a horizontal desire. It took only one waltz, which may on reflection have been a rumba, to convince Destiny of my horizontal desire. I did this by treading on her feet a lot. I think I may have drawn blood. There was no mistaking my message. I dance for keeps.

Words were unnecessary. Nevertheless, as we lurched passionately on the spot, Destiny would murmur little tendernesses into my ear. 'Ow,' she would murmur, or 'Try standing upright,' or 'Do you have to do that?' The other dancers may have been fooled. I wasn't.

Somehow when the dance was done Destiny and I separated. But it didn't matter. We had forged a link that no man could put asunder. Thirst and exhaustion took me first to the bar, then to a remote part of the marquee where gravity was strong. Curled in a canvas corner I drifted into a dream in which I sprinted to the sandpit, soared aloft and came to earth in Albania where I ruled the rugged people with autocratic benevolence.

Suddenly old C.B. was prodding my kidneys again. I rolled over and flicked open an autocratic eye. Someone had glued my tongue to my palate. An Albanian was jabbing me with the nozzle of a vacuum cleaner.

'It's all over, mate,' he said in fluent English. 'Time to go home.' I wandered out into the eerie light of a Christchurch dawn, hailed a cab and went home to sit by the phone and wait for Destiny to call.

The devil's abroad

Travel broadens the mind. For this reason I avoid it. Besides, I have dogs. It is hard to travel with dogs and impossible to put them in kennels. But then last weekend friends asked me to visit with dogs. The dogs could sleep in the house, they said. There was space for them to run. There were no sheep for miles. It sounded too good to be true, but I went.

It was too good be true. There was a goat.

I cannot see the point of goats. Goats eat gorse, socks and plastic with equal pleasure. Truck batteries can run off a goat's digestive juices. Goats smell like goats. Their cheese smells like sewage. Goats butt, kick and look stupid.

In America, Randy is a christian name. Everywhere else, randy is a goat, for people since time began have linked goats with lechery. Lechery is sin, sin is the devil and the devil has goat hooves, goat eyes, goat horns and a vacuous goat grin. It is said that once a day every goat visits the devil to have his beard combed. I believe it.

For obvious reasons, then, I have had little to do with goats. I have had even less to do with horses. Once, however, I had too much to do with both at the same time. It was all the fault of a rich girl called Zippy. She was called Zippy for reasons disappointingly innocent, but she made up for that innocence by having horses. Horses terrify me. They have teeth and nostrils and back legs. One afternoon Zippy asked if I had ever ridden a horse. I coughed modestly and murmured that I had. I was going on to say that I had been six at the time and the horse had been twenty-seven but before you could say terror we were out in the paddock and I was being helped on to a stallion called, if I remember rightly, Bowel-tightener. Bowel-tightener was huge but it accepted me on to its back with ominous calm. When I struggled finally into a sitting position, it still didn't move, nor even when I swivelled to face in the right direction.

'Say "Trot",' said Zippy. I said 'Trot' and to my astonishment, we trotted. I felt like Mark Todd.

I don't know what Mark Todd is like at spotting goats. I'm quite good at it. I spotted the goat on the far side of the paddock almost immediately. Bowel-tightener took five seconds to spot the goat but made up for the delay by launching into an instant gallop goatward. I do not know if the horse was driven by affection or by hatred and at the time I didn't inquire. I was more concerned with screaming. Then the goat went behind a bush. 'What goat where?' said Bowel-tightener's tiny brain to its monstrous body, and the horse stopped. I chose that moment to effect a forward dismount double somersault with one and a half twists: degree of difficulty – a week in bed with Lucozade.

So much then for my acquaintance with goats, until, that is, last weekend when I woke in a bed which I didn't recognize but for the two square metres of dogflesh stretched out over most of it. It was six in the morning. The dogs suggested we go exploring.

The little township was asleep, the air had an autumnal edge, the light was like shattered glass and I felt in dreadful danger of writing poetry. Until, that is, we turned into Goat Street.

It wasn't called Goat Street but it should have been, for on a steep and rugged slope beneath a house on poles, stood a ruminating pot-bellied billy. The dogs dived over the rim and down the slope. They wanted goat. The goat was tethered. One dog barked rampant at the goat's nose, the other at its heels. The goat lowered its head and surged but was brought up short by its tether. The dogs exulted. I whistled them, but might as well have whistled Jesus.

The goat surged again, uprooted its tether and charged the white dog who bounded across the hill, delighted with fright. I shouted. In Goat House a curtain opened and a sleepy accusing face appeared at the window. I waved cheerfully then launched myself into Goat Gulch. The three beasts thundered past me. I slithered down the slope, dived to tackle a dog, grabbed an armful of air and rolled deftly into a boulder. Applause. I looked up to see two women in nightgowns and a man in paisley pyjamas standing on the deck. They were laughing.

I waved and shrugged to the crowd, as if to say

sorry to wake you but you know how it is. One of the women shouted. I did not make out the words but I smiled back as if I did. The goat slammed into the back of my legs. I re-enacted my dismount routine. The boulder had not got any softer.

It wasn't until the man in pyjamas came down to re-tether the goat that I managed to secure the dogs. I drove home that afternoon. Travel is perilous. The devil is abroad. I shall keep to a narrow mind.

Neerg fingers

How excellent to see garden centres being prosecuted for trading over Easter when you and I were busy with God. I should like to see garden centres prosecuted far more often on any pretext whatsoever. They need spraying with a sort of legal herbicide till the garden centre owners with their grubby fingernails and unthinkable underwear finally give up altogether and close down for the greater good of mankind.

I read somewhere – no, it doesn't matter where; frankly it wasn't the sort of publication that I care to be known to have read – that gardening is the preferred leisure activity of about ninety-eight per cent of the population. Anyone who has a 'preferred leisure activity' at all, or indeed anyone who can read the words 'preferred leisure activity' without gagging, is quite beyond redemption and should be condemned to watch *5.30 with Jude* until their kidneys implode. Anyway, if the statistics are even remotely accurate then all hope is lost and our only salvation is anthrax in the water supply.

Yes, yes, I know, you don't have to tell me, I just haven't got the patience or the love of nature to garden. I'm full of angst and arrogance and out of sync with chlorophyll. I simply envy the green-fingered ones.

Well, let me tell you something. I may not be Capability Brown, but I'm as much in touch with nature as the next man. Barely a week goes by without me winding the car window down to get a good deep sniff of the stuff.

On the gardening charge I will confess to having the opposite of green fingers – neerg fingers I suppose – but I have learned to wear my neerginess with pride.

When we neergs plant things they die. One minute they're sitting up all cheerful and bushy in their little plastic nappies on the wet sawdust at the garden centre, the next they're in my garden and instantly horizontal and fermenting the sort of gases that puncture ozone. I used to find it depressing and expensive. Now I don't care. If ever the urge to do a spot of gardening wells up these days I just go out and ram a few twenty-dollar bills into the soil. They're the right colour and it saves on petrol and they don't need watering.

All garden centres – why 'centres' anyway? – should be prosecuted, but there should also be a special prosecutor, a sort of NZ Torquemada, appointed to hunt down and torture the owners of garden centres that sell native plants. Native plants are mind-murderingly drab. They are all called *pittosporum banksii* and they come in green or green. A native plant's idea of flowering is to put out three millimetres of pale green petal beneath a leaf for two days a decade. Note how natives are always planted round shoddy new housing and on the malarial rims of industrial eyesores. They are economy vegetation serving only to mask woven wire fences and oil-soaked, crap-strewn, guard-dog-guarded repositories for lumps of dead engine.

And oh the prejudice of gardeners. They discriminate between plants on utterly spurious grounds. I once heard a large woman define a weed as anything that didn't need her help to grow. That's horticultural apartheid.

What's more, it confirms my suspicion that all gardeners are closet self-flagellants. If dandelions were hard to grow, gardeners would salivate over their dense golden beauty and the ineffable tuftiness of their fruiting pods. But they aren't hard to grow so gardeners get down on their knees with their little dibbers and their dinky little bottles of paraquat and they seek out the innocent little darlings and they kill them.

Neergs don't. We like dandelions. I've now got a 500-square-metre dandelion and dollar-bill farm. It will be open to the public for tours, starting next Easter.

Lies

There we were, dining tête-à-tête in a candlelit restaurant off Manchester Street and things were a bit sticky. She had accused me of, not to put too fine a point on it, lying to her.

I said there were lies everywhere and drew her attention to the oxtail soup. I asked her why, if ox tails were so good, had I never knowingly eaten any other parts of an ox? I said I didn't see the country infested by docked oxen. The answer, of course, is that ox tails are actually cow tails but cowtail soup sounds a bit too nasty because we've all seen cow tails swishing expressively in paddocks, and being, how shall we say, just a little besmeared; so oxtail soup's a lie. Indeed it's such a good lie that butchers fool people with it. 'So you see,' I said with the merest hint of triumph, 'lies are everywhere,' and I called for another bowl of oxtail just to celebrate the great human skill of lying.

Where would we be without lies? There'd be no television news or pop songs or advertisements or any of the things that make life worth living. I went to Czechoslovakia years ago before it became two places that nobody's heard of, back in the good old

235

days when Moscow's merry fist slammed down on any Vladimir who even thought of putting a foot out of line, and Czechoslovakia in those days was not only unspellable but it was also seriously grim. It was all grey concrete and grey snow and bad beer and worse sausages, and it took me a while to work out what was wrong and what was wrong was it lacked lies. There wasn't an ad to be seen, not a single poster telling you that if you used deodorant you'd have to hire a Dobermann to fight the women off, or if you went to Vanuatu everybody would smile at you – not that Czechs could go to Vanuatu because passports were as rare as happiness – and so the poor old downtrodden Czechs just muttered their way around dirty streets eating cabbage, knowing there was no prospect of anything but cabbage tomorrow and so looking truth in the eye and being, in consequence, very sad indeed. What they needed was a sprinkling of lies.

'And of course, darling,' I said to her, 'the irony of the whole thing . . .'

'The what?' she said.

'The irony, darling, irony,' but she hadn't heard of it so I gave up. 'My simple point is, sweetie,' I said, 'that lying is fun and dangerous and human and creative and necessary for the maintenance of sanity. Animals can't do it and we can and there's an end to it. And there's little joy to be got from truth,' I said. 'I mean truth's one of two things: it's either nasty or it's boring or it's false.'

She said that was three things but I swept on.

'First,' I said, 'nasty truth, like we're all going to

die, or being young ought to be good but we spend most of it being miserable, or being old ought to be nasty and is, so we spend it wishing we were young, or time is cruel and all the other stuff of poetry. That's nasty truth,' I said, 'and then there's boring truth which is the grisly details of reality, all the sordid little worries about money and sex, and unsatisfactory washing machines and watching *Coronation Street* and fiddling the income tax and yearning for outdoor furniture from the Warehouse. That's the boring truth,' I said, 'and then there's the false truth.'

'False truth?' she said.

'False truth,' I said, 'like American how-to-become-rich books, or opinion polls or I love you.'

'You do?' she said

'I do,' I said.

I believe

It is a relief to know that the western world is in good hands.

Last week the president of the United States retired to Martha's Vineyard to rebuild his marriage. As any counsellor will tell you, the only way for a wayward husband to make it up to his wife is to play golf with billionaires. So there was Mr Clinton, hacking his way through the rough of Hillary's displeasure, when all of a sudden duty called.

You and I would have told duty to go and wait with a gin in the clubhouse, but neither you nor I are president of the United States. In a fairer world, of course, we would be, but for now the job has gone to the jogger with the chubby legs.

Anyway, last Friday, old Martha was merrily trampling out the vintage when a telegram from the Pentagon comes knocking at the vineyard door. Mr Clinton scans the telegram, drops his three-iron and, with a cry of 'My country needs me' jumps on to the first available intern. Security hauls him off and flies him to Washington.

Mr Clinton has a special voice which he pulls out for the big occasions. He used it to tell us that he

238

hadn't had sex with Monica Lewinsky. He also used it to tell us that he had had sex with Monica Lewinsky. Last week he used it to tell us that America has identified and deployed its full military might against global enemy number one, that threat to life, liberty and the American way, Something Bin Something.

We learned that Mr Bin Something comes from Saudi Arabia and is very rich. Nevertheless he chooses to live in a tent in Afghanistan. This may be because when it comes to terrorism, Afghans take the biscuit, but more likely it is because it makes him into the perfect bogeyman.

CIA intelligence – anyone for oxymoron? – has proved beyond doubt that Mr Bin Something is a terrorist. For a start, they have pointed out that Mr Bin Something wears cloth on his head. This means he's an Arab and probably a relative of Yassir Arafat.

Second, he lives in a place which sounds really suspicious.

Third, he looks like a bit like a Klingon.

Faced with this proof that Mr Bin Something masterminded the embassy bombings, the World Trade Centre bombing, the Lockerbie plane crash, the Californian earthquake and the AIDS epidemic, it was clear that the United States of America had to act. Furthermore it was vital to act last Friday for a multitude of reasons which the CIA has listed and which I will quote in full.

1. The president had just admitted having sex with Monica Lewinsky.

So President Clinton ordered his navy to fire missiles on to the sovereign territory of other countries. There used to be a word for this robust style of diplomacy. That word was war.

After World War Two the world created the United Nations to stop war. It has done an excellent job except when countries have decided to go to war. Also, because it has lots more weapons than anyone else and it owes lots of money to the United Nations, America has always felt free to invade anyone it likes whenever it likes.

So the missiles flew and *One Network News'* team coverage treated us to exciting pictures of simulated missiles cruising over simulated bits of Africa and the Middle East. In deepest Sudan they blew up an aspirin factory. As the aspirins rained from the sky every Sudanese with a headache rejoiced, apart, that is, from the Sudanese who were in the factory. Their headaches took a turn for the worse.

The CIA had two excellent reasons to bomb the factory:

1. It had been manufacturing nerve gas.

2. The president had just admitted having sex with Monica Lewinsky.

The Sudanese have protested to the United Nations. That will do them a lot of good. What they haven't done is to express any worry about the deadly chemicals which have presumably been showered over Khartoum. I find this surprising.

Meanwhile America approves of the bombing. Even though Mr Clinton spent last week owning up to lies, eighty per cent of Americans have apparently believed his story about Mr Bin Something and the aspirin factory.

Mr Bin Something will soon have served his purpose whereupon he will fade quietly away and leave not a wrack behind. A year from now his name will mean nothing.

Meanwhile, however, Madeleine Albright has warned the American people to be vigilant. Retaliation could come at any moment. I will be a little less than surprised if that moment coincides with the publication of a report by a certain Mr Starr.

Forget *Wag the Dog*. Has anyone here read *Nineteen Eighty-four*?

Knickers

Mr William Geddie's twentieth century differed from mine.

As you may know, Mr William Geddie MA edited the *Chambers Twentieth Century Dictionary* and it was to him that I turned last week to look up the word 'knickers'. You don't need to know why. Anyway, Mr Geddie informed me that knicker-bockers were women's undergarments gathered at the knee, but of knickers he said nothing at all.

Under 'knicker' he told me to go to 'nicker'. I went, and found that a nicker is a water-monster. It is also a Scottish laugh and a round seed used for playing marbles, all of which are great fun but awkward under a skirt. In Mr Geddie's twentieth century knickers didn't exist.

But I don't know what else to call women's undergarments. Bloomers are a joke, undies in-fantile, pants trousers, underpants male and panties twee.

Lingerie sings of silken self-indulgence, but no one can pronounce it except the French and, as every schoolboy knows, French women don't wear knickers.

The most signal truth about knickers is that women need to own about a hundred pairs, i.e. one for every pair of shoes. Of the women I have known well, both had a drawer so crammed with knickers that when you hauled it open the things sprang at you.

For years we men have watched the female fascination with underwear with baffled curiosity. But now the tables are turning, for of late the manufacturers of underwear have swung the ruthless spotlight of their advertising on to men.

Today as I drove to work I was confronted by a man recumbent on a billboard. His hair was long, his smile laconic, body bronzed and muscles taut. Amidships he sported a pair of lime-green underpants. They were called Hunks. The Hunks harboured a squid.

In Mr Geddie's day men's underpants went unconsidered except for the weekly change of yellowing Y-fronts. This change was like the peeling of skin. But now in every menswear shop there stands a rack of brand-name underwear. Each is advertised by the mandatory youth with a flopping fringe and the figure of a Greek discus thrower.

And the advertising works. Having checked that there is no one we know at the checkout, we buy our Hunks, Chunks or Woppers and we bear them home like contraband. In the privacy of the bedroom we cram ourselves into them and pose before the mirror in the manner of body-builders.

What we seek is youth. What we see is sagging

dugs and missing muscles. We shake what is left of our hair. The dandruff falls like a Christmas paperweight and weary with disillusion we cram the underpants into the back of a drawer like a letter from abroad that we will never answer.

For as the commercial world turns its attention increasingly to men, exhorting us to groom ourselves, to spray ourselves, to care how we appear, we of the playdough bellies are learning at last how women have felt all these years; we are learning the humiliation of imperfection.

I think, on balance, I prefer Mr Geddie's twentieth century to my own.

Agley

'The best laid plans of mice and men', said Robbie Burns, 'gang aft agley', a truism which has reminded countless generations of the folly of trying to understand the Scots.

I was reminded of the expression the other day by Margaret. 'You have to go to Auckland,' Margaret had said, 'for an interview.'

My heart swelled like a cabbage.

'Auckland?' I exclaimed. 'That cosmopolitan metropolis where life travels at breakneck speed and whose streets are paved with the corpses of those who couldn't keep up?'

Margaret got caught up in my excitement. 'Yes,' she said.

'Hot diggety dawg,' I said.

Suppressing her joy behind a frosty brow, Margaret handed me my travel plans. I danced a jig of joy which involved the adroit headbutting of a fluorescent tube.

'Leave it,' said Margaret, 'I'll clean it up. Remember the interview is early in the morning. It's important. Stay off the booze and don't be late.'

'Never fear,' I exclaimed.

It was then that Margaret quoted Robbie Burns, whereupon I chuckled a nonchalant chuckle, waved a nonchalant wave and headed home to lay plans.

I arranged to stay with Gareth in a bijou apartmentette in Remuera where I arrived in the late afternoon. Gareth was out, so I headed into Remmers to test the waters. By chance I met Gareth in the street, and he urged me to share a water with him.

'No no,' I exclaimed, 'call me Goody Two-Shoes but I have to be up early in the morning, perky as a perky thing.'

'Heineken?' asked Gareth.

'Thank you,' I said, and we fell to watching the sea of tanned bodies and black dresses that washed along Remuera Road like a costly tide. The women were well dressed too, but soon it was time for me to leave for dinner with a former colleague whose life has taken her from the swamps of Christchurch to the plateau of Parnell.

'I'll not be late back,' I told Gareth.

'The key's on the windowsill,' he said.

Friday night in Parnell and the recession was in full swing. Gloomy patrons spilled on to the pavement from every bar and restaurant, weeping noisily into their Bollinger. After a wait of barely an hour we secured a table in an Italian joint where I was all abstemiousness. Having wrung the dregs from bottle three, I kissed my former colleague goodbye smack on midnight, poured myself into a taxi and returned to Remmers.

The key was on the windowsill, and a bed had

been laid out on the living room floor, along with an alarm clock and a thoughtful little packet of aspirins. The window looked out over a garden where the neighbour was winding up an alfresco dinner party by playing the accordion. It was unreasonable behaviour and I opened the window to remonstrate.

'Oi,' I remonstrated, 'may I join you?'

The neighbour, it transpired, lived in one of those freaky time zones. Though I stayed less than an hour it was five o'clock when I got in. When I say 'got in' I mean that I reached the door at five. The windowsill was bare. Roused by my merry knocking Gareth was all smiles. He was also all smiles a little while later when he came into the living room and invited me to turn the alarm off.

I glanced at the clock, took a leisurely ten-second shower, a handful of aspirins and a spoonful of peanut butter, and sprinted for a taxi. Fifteen minutes later, as I awaited the interview, I decided that the peanut butter had been an error of judgement.

At Christchurch airport Margaret asked me how the interview had gone. I groped for the apt words but they eluded me, just as, I dimly remembered, they had in the interview. But then I struck gold.

'Agley,' I said, 'it ganged agley.'

Margaret managed to conceal her mirth behind a frosty silence.

Angels and warthogs

Pablo Picasso could draw like an angel. I have seen film of Picasso drawing a bull on a guitar. He captured the essence of bull in a single line.

His was a glorious gift, for to make art is to reach for something beyond ourselves. It is to snatch at eternity. It is what makes us human.

But for some reason Picasso the angel spent most of his life drawing like a warthog. Of course Picasso was free to do as he wished with his talent, but I find it hard to forgive him his legacy. More than any other painter, Picasso the warthog must take the blame for the tosh that infests most modern art galleries, tosh produced by painters who are long on warthog but short on angel. When I start my aesthetic revolution, and the time is drawing near, these artists will be the first against the wall.

In his private life Picasso was neither warthog nor angel. He was a lusty soul who attracted a stream of wives and mistresses. Quite why artists attract women I don't know. Perhaps the women sniff eternity. Or good sex. Or both.

Anyway, with the gallantry typical of the Spanish caballero, Picasso painted his womenfolk. In homage to their charms he painted portraits which made them look like geometry with eyes. The eyes fell in strange places. Most of the women left soon after they were painted.

One of these women has just died and a London auction house has sold her collection of Picasso stuff. There were many paintings. There were also doodles and other Picasso trivia. The auction grossed $60m. Among the buyers, one lucky bidder parted with only a few hundred dollars and scuttled into the night clutching to his or her breast a paper napkin torn by the hand of the master himself into the shape of what may or may not be a ferret.

What I want to ask is, Why? Why did someone pay money for a napkin that had been clumsily torn by a drunken Spaniard for his lover sixty years ago?

On one level the answer is obvious – the man who tore the napkin was Picasso. On another level it is less obvious. A torn napkin is a torn napkin. That it was torn by Picasso does not make it art. It doesn't even make it well torn.

Imagine that someone managed to prove that the napkin had come from McDonald's and had been torn by one of those scrofular youths who ask you if you want fries even though you didn't ask for fries. The napkin's value would drain instantly to zilch.

So, the napkin's value lies purely in its association with Picasso. This reminds me of nothing so much as the medieval world, when there was big money in religious relics. Churches around Europe held enough pieces of the true cross to build an ark.

They supplemented these with such splendid trophies as the tibia of Mary Magdalene or, honestly, the Relic of the Holy Circumcision. There were three of these.

Today we laugh at such mummery. But every purchase of a miniskirt worn by Ginger Spice, a microphone licked by Hendrix, or a napkin torn by Picasso shows the same instinct at work in a secular age. It is a vain snatch at eternity by association. And it doesn't work.

Could do better

One purpose of a school report is to tell the parents how their child is doing at school. An equally important purpose is to make the teacher look good.

If a child performs poorly parents tend to blame the teacher. Teachers don't like to be blamed so they mask the problem with words. 'Anthony is easily distracted' means he doesn't do any work. 'Anthony's attention span could be improved' means he doesn't do any work. 'Anthony has organizational problems' means he doesn't bring any books.

My own school reports of thirty years ago were simple affairs. I still have one from the fourth form. Under each subject there's a percentage figure and a comment. I was a swot. Physics says 'good'. Latin says 'chatterbox'. All the other say 'sound progress'. The headmaster, a man of flair, put the incisive personal touch to the report by writing the only complete sentence. 'Bennett is making sound progress,' he wrote.

Reports like these came on a single sheet of paper. Teachers like these reports because they can see what everyone else has written. If six other teachers write that Blank is keen and diligent, it does not pay to write that Blank farts and fights. Blank's wind and wounds become the teacher's fault.

Many school reports these days are written, however, on separate sheets which are then collated into a booklet. These present the teacher with two problems. The first is that they provide too much space to fill. The second is that the teachers are writing in isolation.

Many teachers resort to the noble arts of bombast and euphemism. Modern educational jargon comes in handy here, the sort of jargon that NZQA produces by the ream and which makes as much sense as the Roswell Incident. With practice a teacher can learn to spout mounds of the stuff. 'This term we have focused on listening skills. Jemima has learned to process aural information from a range of authentic contexts and has gained a satisfactory grasp of the concepts involved.'

The computer helps here. Once a teacher has created a magnificent sentence like this he can cut and paste it on to every report at the touch of a key.

On several occasions in my teaching career I have seen phantom reports. These are reports for pupils who have long since left the school but somehow remained in the records. Administration has churned out a blank report for the child and teachers have filled it in. Most of the teachers report that the non-existent student, though quiet in class, has worked steadily. Once, however, a magnificently incompetent geography teacher in Canada, made a point of praising the lively contribution to class discussion made by a boy who had died in the holidays.

In almost twenty years of teaching I have written about 10,000 reports. I am proud of two of them. One said simply 'yes'. The headmaster sent it back to me.

The other occurred in the days of single-page reports. It did not pay to make an error on such a report because it meant that every teacher had to rewrite his comment. This particular report was for a boy called James. Someone distracted me as I went to write. In consequence I began my report, 'David . . .' It was the end of term and half the teachers had already gone home. I couldn't possibly force a rewrite.

'David eventually slew Goliath,' I wrote, 'and James might finally master spelling.' The comment bore no relation to James' performance, but that, of course, didn't matter at all. It was a splendid report.

From here to prostate

I was pretending to read a plastic picture-card telling me how to jump out of the plane, but surreptitiously I was scanning the passengers coming down the aisle for the one who would sit next to me. I have a gift for attracting the seriously religious and mothers with psychotic infants. Somehow you always know who's going to sit beside you the moment you see them. Perhaps it's the dangling saliva.

She had to squeeze past me to get to the window seat. Aeroplane friendship always begin with your eyes about eight inches from the other's crotch, the sort of position it can take a normal friendship a good month to attain, if ever. Such instant proximity can break the ice, of course. It can also thicken it.

'These seats are made for anorexics,' she said. I could detect no hint of religion in the sentence, and if there was a psychotic infant then she had stowed it in the overhead locker, which was just fine by me. On Bennett Airlines, all children travel as freight.

Anyway, as opening comments go this one

seemed to go pretty well. I decided to risk a flight's-worth of evangelism by an expansive gesture of friendship. I flicked an eyebrow and expelled a little air through one nostril. It's one of my more effective come-ons.

Two minutes later I had tucked the picture-card back in that nifty little seat pocket and was ignoring the safety pantomime starring a bored stewardess and an implausible oxygen mask that is attached to nothing but which one is supposed to tug. There's no point in watching it. Just as I know that I like Guinness, have never grown up and can't stop smoking, so I know with equal certainty that in the event of an air accident I would exhibit without hesitation my talent for panic.

But this was not why I was ignoring the panto on this occasion. Rather my attention was held elsewhere, for beside me, I had discovered, was sitting a creature whom I had never thought about before but whom, if I had ever got round to thinking about her, I would have presumed not to exist.

Barbara, for that was her name – well, actually it wasn't. I can't quite remember her name but I think it had the same number of syllables – lived in Southland, which of course is nothing remarkable – several people have been doing it for years and don't seem much the worse for the experience – but the extraordinary thing is that Barbara, or rather 'Barbara', made her living down there where the nights are long and the grass longer, by selling, wait for it, vitamins.

I think I had better repeat that, without any of

those interruptions which seems to be creeping into the sentences today – not that I mind them, of course, in fact I think they add a ring of authenticity, the stamp of a mind in action, don't you think? – anyway, Barbara, or rather 'Barbara', (you're with me? good) sold vitamins, which she pronounced *vi*tamins whereas I was brought up to say *vit*amins, not that it makes much difference I suppose, in Southland. Is that clearer now? Have you latched on to the full import of that statement?

Now, I'm no Ranulph Fiennes, but I have been to Southland. Last year. January. High summer. Gore. Sunday afternoon. It was raining. Hard.

The main street of Gore was wide and wet – and empty but for two elderly men on stationary old-fashioned bicycles about ten feet apart outside the Four Square Superstore which was, astonishingly, closed. Both elderly men were wearing brown overcoats and cycle clips. Neither elderly man was looking at the other elderly man. Both elderly men were using battered vegetable knives to slash at their wrists.

All of the above is true apart from the bit about the vegetable knives. They may have been chisels. It was hard to tell at that distance and unfortunately the photos didn't come out. I needed a flash.

Anyway, that's all I know of Southland. So when 'Barbara' said she sold *vi*tamins down there I thought of the two elderly men and I thought ah-ha and I said, eloquently, 'Oh.' And as if that wasn't enough I added, 'So, how's business?'

'Booming,' said 'Barbara'.

I have never been one to fear repetition. If the word is right, use it as many times as you like. So I said, 'Oh' again.

'Barbara' looked me up and down. I could hardly begrudge her this look given my earlier intimacy with her crotch. She took in my thinning hair, and the other one that isn't thinning quite so badly. She took in my hammer toes. 'You need zinc,' she said.

We then had a witty little interchange about zinc. It went like this:

'Zinc?'

'Zinc.'

'Zinc?'

'Zinc.'

'Oh.'

Already half convinced I asked her why I needed zinc. 'Barbara' insisted that all men need zinc. It fixes everything.

'Everything?'

'From here to prostate.'

I immediately knew that I had got from this trip, if nothing else, the ideal title for every man's autobiography. I told her so.

'No,' said 'Barbara', 'from *hair* to prostate.'

'Oh,' I said, 'well, that's not bad either.'

She laughed. I laughed. We laughed all the way to Auckland. The flight took about ten minutes. She was a charming woman. But then she would have to be to sell vitamins in Gore.

Not that I'm a convert to vitamins, you understand. I will admit to having had, since my return,

257

a nibble or two at a galvanized hinge on the laundry door, but that's only because there's nothing to lose. Soon hair will be a memory and the prostate prostrate. And then you jump out of the plane.

Baking nuts

There comes a time on a Sunday when the body craves something more substantial than aspirins. And it was at just this time last Sunday that I read an article about baking biscuits.

Grandmothers bake biscuits; I don't. I have never filled my tins.

But the article featured a recipe for gingernuts. I love gingernuts. Bite into a dry one and it's an even-money bet whether tooth or biscuit will break first. Dunk a gingernut in coffee, however, and it becomes a delicious confection which is easily spooned from the bottom of the cup. I read the recipe, I salivated and I decided I would bake.

Having ransacked the larder for ingredients, I rang a woman who knows. She told me that no, I couldn't really do without eggs or ground ginger. Nor could I substitute noodles for flour or beer for golden syrup.

I had to have baking soda too, apparently, but she reassured me that even if I never baked another biscuit my baking soda would not go to waste. I could clean the bath with it.

The woman who knows doesn't know my bath.

Anything that could clean that bath has no business in biscuits. It would be more at home in a warhead.

My trip to the supermarket cost me a smidgin under $15. I calculated that my homebaking would power into profit after 500 biscuits.

In measuring 100 grams of butter the bathroom scales proved unsatisfactory, but all great cooks are innovators. On the 27th of July 1975 I took six wickets for forty-seven against Eastbourne, and was presented with the ball. It has travelled round the world with me.

A cricket ball weighs five and a half ounces. I tickled the calculator and found I needed two thirds of a cricket ball of butter, one and half cricket balls of sugar and one and three quarters of flour.

After that it was a simple matter of placing the cricket ball in a bowl in the right hand and ingredients in a bowl in the left hand and seeing which way I leaned.

I had to cream the sugar and butter. I presumed that cream meant beat. Creaming proved an efficient method of bending forks.

After five minutes' creaming I had whipped up an armful of lactic acid and the dogs had whipped up an enthusiasm for airborne lumps of sugared butter.

Add one tbsp of gold syrup. Golden syrup is not divisible into tbsps. It is not divisible into anything. However high you lift your tbsp it remains linked to the golden syrup tin by a rope of sagging sweetness. In the end the dogs solved the rope problem.

Sifting one and three quarter cricket balls of flour

from a height proved to be fun. Some of the flour landed in the bowl. Rather more landed on my black dog. When she sneezed she looked like the inside of a Christmas paperweight.

Creaming time again, then a pause to revive the creaming arm and straighten the creaming fork, before rolling the sludge into twenty-four golfballs and laying them on the baking tray I hadn't got. Improvising with tin-foil was genius, but transferring the foil to the oven proved costly. Balls roll. The dogs got seven of them raw.

Then all I had to do was turn the light on in the oven, pull up a chair and watch my balls become nuts. They sweated a little, then slowly, beautifully, they darkened. As the biscuits flattened, I swelled. As the surfaces cracked like the picture in the recipe I burst with pride.

Twenty-five minutes later I drew from the oven seventeen perfect gingernuts. I laid them on the wire cooling tray known as the kitchen bench, and dashed to the phone to boast to the woman who knows. She was out.

Having hauled the dogs off the bench I cooled the eleven gingernuts by blowing on them. Then I picked one up. It was as hard as an ice-hockey puck, a toothbuster, the real thing. I made a coffee. I dunked the biscuit. It disintegrated. I did a little jig. After forty-one years I had filled my tins.

Twenty Yak

There comes a moment in the life of any smoker when he knows with sudden certainty that he will never smoke another cigarette. This moment normally occurs in hospital and is followed by a dramatic fall in body temperature.

When I enter *Mastermind*, smoking will be my specialist topic. I took up smoking at just the right age and did not, as so many of my contemporaries did, give up when we moved to secondary school. I also smoked for all the right reasons; viz., sex, sport and poverty. Anyone who knows me now will confirm my prowess in just over thirty per cent of these. In other words, then, I reckon I know a thing or two about smoking.

That, however, was until today. For today I rang the editor of *The Press*. I'll rephrase that. Today I rang THE EDITOR OF *THE PRESS*, an august gentleman, immune to capital-letter flattery and sporting one of those Frank Nobilo beards of stubble which I've never quite understood. What I don't understand is how they tend them. Is there some sort of shaver like a ride-on mower that is sold only to golfers and prominent, stately editors who are no doubt also nifty with the five-iron?

Anyway THE EDITOR OF *THE PRESS* and I got chatting, as one does with editors, about cigarettes, and HE said some frightfully kind things about my rate of consumption. Was HE a smoker, I asked. It turned out that THE EDITOR OF *THE PRESS* was an ex-smoker, which I've always thought, as I told HIM, to be the very best type of smoker. How, I asked, did he stop? And HE said, 'Yak.'

See what a pithy man HE is. Yak. It's a beautiful answer. Economical, trenchant, enigmatic, editory. I was impressed. THE EDITOR OF *THE PRESS* didn't get where HE is today by beating about the bush. Ask HIM a straight question and HE'll say, 'Yak.'

It transpired that Yak is a brand of Nepalese cigarette popular with the more suicidal Sherpas. A few beards ago THE EDITOR OF *THE PRESS* was in Nepal – well-travelled too, you see – and faced with a cash-flow crisis. American cigarettes were beyond his pocket and Yak, though less than a dong for a packet of twenty, were, as HE put it, 'guaranteed tonsilitis'. So HE gave up. Just like that. There's character. There's strength. There's what this country needs a bit more of. And that's exactly what I told HIM, in a most unobsequious man-to-man way.

But for those of us who flounder a little lower on the evolutionary ladder than editors, stopping smoking is less straightforward. I've had a dab or two at it myself. I could never get a decent drag out

263

of those patch things, and the chewing gum stuff was so bitter that I had to have a coffee to take the taste away, and as even the simplest chemist knows, Coffee grounds + H_2O (heated) = Unquenchable lust for a cigarette.

Of course, one can go the organic route. I have in front of me the 'Wise Woman's Tips For Giving Up Smoking'. They include, 'Bring home a flower', 'Eat a wild salad – even if it's only one dandelion leaf', and, top of the list, 'Take an oat-straw bath'. All great fun as I am sure you agree, but in my 'garden' it's hard to know if you've got to the dandelion before the dogs have, so I just brought a flower home and ate it. This necessitated a coffee to take the taste away.

Sprawled in my oat-straw bath with *The Press* and twenty Rothmans I saw an ad in the personal column. 'Stop smoking the easy way . . . Hypnosis.'

Now, I owe a lot to my mother. She taught me how to know when a sponge is cooked, which strangers to accept lifts from (the wealthy ones), and a method of gripping the carotid artery that I have never seen bettered. (On the famous night when she caught the burglar *in flagrante* and the spare bedroom, the police had to ring around for his dental records.)

What my mother never told me, however, and finding it out for myself has cost me time, money and tears, was to shun all people with framed diplomas on the wall.

The hypnotist's wall was more diplomas than wall. Pride of place went to an ornate little number reading, 'The Bulawayo Centre for Hypnosis, Naturopathy and Proctoscopy. Weekend residential course. Pass with distinction.' It had a big red seal.

I paid $70 to the hypnotist, who was wearing a golf-club sweater but didn't have a proper beard, and then I conned him. I did this by pretending to be hypnotized when I wasn't. I closed my eyes and breathed slowly and spoke robotically. He was completely taken in.

The moment it was over I went straight round to the dairy for twenty Yak. They were out of Yak, so I had to settle for Camel on the grounds of their similar exotic shagginess, and then I lounged against a lamppost opposite the hypnotist's diploma-laden house and smoked ostentatiously. It was one of those moments of triumph, rather like talking man-to-man and straight up with THE EDITOR OF *THE PRESS*. Such things make life worth living.

Plane greetings

There was a toddler at the airport. The toddler seemed to have two mothers. Neither of them seemed to like him much. The toddler was entertaining those of us who were waiting in the terminal by ramming us with a luggage-trolley. When one or other of his mothers told him off he entertained us further by wailing.

I had come to greet friends from Canada. Travelling is harrowing, and after a long flight people should not have to deal alone with the rigours of a foreign airport. I like to give them a warm, human, southern welcome and to help them carry their duty-free goods.

I had also come to inspect the new international terminal since my invitation to the gala opening went astray in the post. I am pleased to report that the new terminal has every appearance of an airport terminal. The architects, Messrs Bland, Synthetic and Pastel, have built a terminal which would merge indistinguishably into any airport in the world.

Travel is traumatic. It wrenches us from the familiar, strips us of the homes and possessions that identify us. You can see on the faces of travellers that they are vulnerable, like hermit crabs scuttling between shells. Perhaps it is to soothe the traveller that all airports are built of the same materials which I cannot name but which owe nothing to nature. Technology whisks the traveller round the globe and squirts him out into the same air-conditioning, automatic plate-glass doors, wiry carpet and recessed lighting that he left in Los Angeles or London, Bangkok or Budapest.

When passengers finally emerge through the doors that say 'Welcome to Christchurch' they find themselves in an identity parade. Several hundred pairs of eyes look up to take them in. It's a hostile welcome.

Every international flight carries the same human freight. The pilots appear first, striding manfully with their natty overnight bags, their uniforms, and their deep smug tans. Then come the stewardesses, their professional manner relaxed a little but still decked out like dolls in national dress. After them the passengers.

The young travel like snails with gargantuan backpacks. If they fall over they can't get up. They do not expect to be greeted. They travel not to enjoy but to endure. They stagger through the terminal and seek out the backpackers' minibus with its hard cheap seats.

Returning tourists are boisterous. They sport unfortunate shirts, Hawaiian hats and suntans that have happened too suddenly.

Middle-aged couples are not boisterous. The

husband pushes the trolley of luggage and the wife steadies it with a single hand, perhaps to retain contact with her identity, or to ward off thieves in a strange land or to ensure that her man doesn't bolt. He doesn't look like bolting.

Few people greet well. Our lives are placid and we are ill-suited to the drama of separation or reunion. The high voltage of emotion discomforts us. Some lovers wrap round each other like vines, but most plant awkward inaccurate kisses and then look at their shoes. Men greet men with a clumsy one-armed embrace which doubles as a backslap.

And when the greetings are over, everyone talks about what the weather has been like.

The toddler, I discovered, did not have two mothers. He had three. The third was his real mum who had been to Sydney. When she appeared through the glass doors her eyes found her baby instantly. She abandoned her trolley and ran to her little piece of flesh. The little piece ran towards her, then stopped and ducked behind a chair. He pouted. He was telling her off for deserting him.

She knelt and spread her arms wide. She was crying. The little monster held off for a few cruel seconds and then the pull grew too strong and he hurtled into her arms as if by suction and exploded into tears. His legs wrapped around her ribs like a chimp's legs. His arms circled her neck and he sank his face into her hair. Mother and son fitted together like pieces of a jigsaw puzzle. And they stayed where they were, entwined and rocking, a Henry Moore statue made flesh, oblivious to the world. Soldiers could not have separated them.

I heard mother promise her child that she would never ever go away again, and then, like his two other mothers and everyone else, I had to turn away because in the midst of the sterile airport terminal I found my eyes were pricking.

At that point my Canadian friends arrived and were so moved by my obvious emotion at seeing them that they gave me a bottle of Scotch and 200 cigarettes and simply refused to hear of payment.

A *thumb in the air*

My favourite short story is called 'Annie' by Jim Crace. The narrator is hitching from solitude in Nevada to his wife in New York and gets a lift in a stolen car. The car's called Annie. The driver's a crim on the run. Neither driver nor narrator has money for gas, so they pick up hitchhikers who chip in a few dollars. When the driver suspects that one of the hitchhikers has rumbled him, he runs away in the night and they drive on without him. The cast of hitchhikers in the car keeps changing. When the narrator reaches New York he leaves Annie to its occupants. Years later he sees Annie again in Louisiana. It's still full of people.

I thought of the story today because I picked up a hitchhiker. She was seventeen, pretty and she wore jeans in the way that only seventeen-year-old girls can wear jeans. That helped of course, but had she been seventeen stone and armed I would have picked her up because I have taken a vow.

For ten years of my life I hitched everywhere. What prompted me to hitch was that most primitive, simple and honourable of human urges, poverty. It wasn't until I was twenty-eight that I bought my first car, the Whale. It cost me six pints of Bass and a prawn curry. On the day I acquired it, I vowed I would not drive past a hitchhiker and I have kept my vow except for people with beards, be they men or women.

The girl wanted to go to New Brighton.

'Hop in,' I said. She scanned the two large and slavering dogs in the back seat. She scanned the empty passenger seat beside me. She got in the back. The dogs were thrilled.

She spoke little. All I could get out of her was that she worked in a pizza parlour. Her silence may have stemmed from the dogs trying to lick her into submission, but that silence reminded me of an unsavoury lad I went to school with, called Pete Thrale.

When we left school, Pete and I went our separate ways: I to university, Pete to any place he could rob. But five years later we met on a motorway intersection near Cricklewood. Pete was waving a huge cardboard arm with the legend 'Entertaining Hitchhikers Ltd'. We got a lift within minutes, whereupon Pete folded his cardboard arm, stuffed it in his rucksack, climbed into the back seat of the car and went to sleep. It was left to me to make conversation with the driver, a sales rep for Marmite, as far as Leeds where he was attending a conference called 'Spreading the Spreads'.

Pete was heading on to Scotland, but we stayed an hour in Leeds, had a beer together, rediscovered our mutual dislike, then went our separate ways once more, this time for ever. But before we did,

Pete gave me a jar of Marmite. He hated the stuff, he said.

Hitching's like that. It's random, shapeless, thrilling and boring in turns. No two journeys are the same. It's also the nearest thing there is to practical socialism. Nevertheless it's a very good thing. The poor get a free ride; the rich get company. Everyone wins.

People will tell you that hitch hiking is dangerous. It is. People die hitchhiking. But they also die on the lavatory, in front of the television or *in flagrante delicto*.

The danger of hitchhiking is that crazy people pick you up. The glory of hitchhiking, on the other hand, is that crazy people pick you up. I remember a Frenchman with a battered Citroën and a face like an aubergine.

I said I wanted to go to Angoulême.

'Oh really,' he said, 'my mother's in hospital in Angoulême. Get in.'

I said I was sorry about his mother and we discussed her condition. I tried him on other topics but none interested him. When I ran out of mother-questions we fell silent.

At a turn-off to Bordeaux, which lay 200km to the south-west, a boy and a girl were hitching. Monsieur Aubergine stopped. The boy and the girl said they wanted to go to Bordeaux.

'Oh really,' said Monsieur Aubergine, 'my mother's in hospital in Bordeaux. Get in.'

Then he told me to get out because I was boring. I walked through midday heat into Angoulême and found a man asleep on a park bench with a lead draped loosely on his arm. At the business end of the lead, and also asleep, lay an adult male lion.

As I have said, hitching's like that. By nature I am neither brave nor adventurous, but hitching thrust adventures on me. No other activity has given me such stories, such horror, such wonder, such fear, such raw and random life.

I drive little these days, but I seem to see fewer hitchhikers on the road every year. Perhaps the young have cars now, perhaps the safety sermons have got to them, I don't know, but the girl from Brighton was the first hitchhiker I have picked up for six months. When we stopped by the pier and she peeled the dogs off, thanked me and walked for ever into somewhere else, I was stabbed by nostalgia and by envy.

Wise fools

I have got into the habit of getting older, and the older I get the more I relish the oxymoron.

I came to the oxymoron late in life and at first I struggled to believe that such a luscious word existed. But exist it does, deriving from the Greek *oxys*, meaning sharp, and *moros*, foolish. Thus it means something pointedly foolish, an apparent contradiction, the sort of thing a fool might say which makes no literal sense but which approaches the truth more nearly than something a wise man might say. Hurry slowly is an example.

Shakespeare knew all about oxymorons. He had Juliet tell Romeo that parting is such sweet sorrow and we haven't stopped saying it since. Shakespeare's fools are among his wisest characters. The fool in *King Lear* sees through every other character in the play. The fool is weak and strong, funny and sad, loving and bitter. He's an oxymoron in motley.

Conversely many of Shakespeare's wise men are fools; Polonius tells us,

This above all – to thine own self be true,

And it must follow, as the night the day,
Thou canst not then be false to any man.

High counsel from the lips of a dingbat, a man
stuffed with vanity, pompous as a dowager and
scheming as a rat. When Polonius finally collects a
sword through the arras and gurgles his life away
we rejoice every bit as much as we grieve.

Cue another oxymoron, *schadenfreude*, a
typically tuneful term from that Lego-language
German, meaning joy at another's distress. How we
would like to deny *schadenfreude* but the ratings
tell the real story. For what is it that over a third of
the population seeks when it turns on the television
at six o'clock each evening if it is not the thrill of
other people's suffering? It is not information; you
will find better information in the pub. Indeed, the
very phrase 'television news' is an oxymoron.

No, we watch the news to see the mother of three
weep at their funeral. We watch it to see the
relatives of kidnap victims turn the mournful pages
of the photograph album and, if we are lucky,
collapse before the camera's cyclopean, dis-
passionate eye. We watch it to see the missiles fired
from the USS *Wallopem* in the Adriatic and we
want to see them land. Though we may con
ourselves with a moral stance, with the tut-tuts of
sympathy, side by side on the sofa with our better
nature sits Sister Schadenfreude, whispering that
we are oxymorons too.

Oxymorons are easy to invent – I think immediately of National Party Think-tank, or committee

decision, or Black Cap victory or the *Australian Journal of Philosophy* – but there is no need to invent oxymorons, for they surround us at every instant of our lives. Fun run is an oxymoron. Parliamentary debate is an oxymoron. President Clinton is an oxymoron. Health service, keeping a secret, moderate drinking, true love, Grey Power, 99% fat-free, modern art, Pacific Ocean, Happy Christmas – the list is endless.

Alexander Pope, the eighteenth-century poet, best summarizes why that list is endless. Pope was stunted and malformed – he couldn't stand erect without a heavy-duty corset – and yet he towered above his contemporaries. He was peevish and venomous and yet he attained a sweetness of voice and a clarity of mind that few can rival.

Himself an oxymoron, Pope wrote of mankind in oxymoronic terms. He called man 'a being darkly wise and rudely great'. He said we were 'born but to die, and reasoning but to err', that we were,

> Created half to rise, and half to fall;
> Great lord of all things, yet a prey to all;
> Sole judge of truth, in endless error hurled:
> The glory, jest and riddle of the world.

And so it is, in this mad and lovely life, that the oxymoron, which makes no sense, makes sense.

Joe Bennett was born in Brighton and since
leaving Cambridge University has taught
English in a variety of countries including
Canada, Spain and New Zealand. He lives
in Christchurch, New Zealand.